LIGHTHOUSE
LEGENDS & HAUNTINGS

Oil Painting by Ron Goyette

"Annie C. Maguire - Portland Head Light"
Shipwrecked December 24, 1886

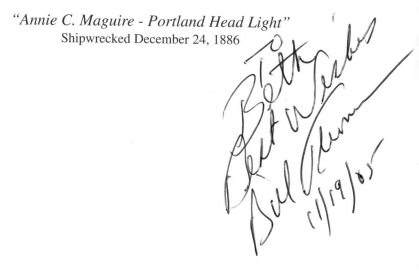

This book is dedicated to the lighthouse keeper's wife

Connie Small

*As with many American lighthouse keepers, her
lighthouse experiences were filled with dignity and beauty. She
experienced isolation, intrigue, romance, and danger. She now
is devoting her life to the preservation and humanitarian work
of keeping the lighthouse spirit alive, the spirit of lighted beacons
bringing hope, trust, and security to all of mankind.*

*Author's Note: Just before this edition was
printed, Mrs. Connie Small passed away on
January 25, 2005 at the age of 103.*

LIGHTHOUSE LEGENDS & HAUNTINGS

By
William O. Thomson

Cover Painting & Oil Paintings
by Ron Goyette

Edited by William M. Thomson

Personal Photographs By
Connie Small
Brenda Ahlgren
Andrew R. Thomson

Line Drawing by Claudia Crafts

'Scapes Me
135 Alewive Road
Kennebunk, Maine 04043

TABLE OF CONTENTS

Dedication   2
Foreword   5
A Tribute to the Legendary Keepers   7
Connie Small   10
Ken Black   31
World War II   38
Nubble Light   42
Brenda Ahlgren's Memories   49
Portland Head   61
Lighthouse Hauntings   67
Seguin Light   69
Ram Island   73
Isles of Shoals   74
Minots Ledge   77
Owls Head   79
Block Island (Southeast)   81
Wood Island   83
Hendricks Head   85
New London Ledge   86
Boon Island   88
Conclusion   92
Author & Artists   93
Bibliography   94

FOREWORD

Lighthouses as we know them will never be built again. In this age of solar power, global positioning systems and automatic fog sensors, all but one of the light stations operated by the United States Coast Guard are fully automated. Constructed mostly by hand from wood, bricks and stones, the old structures are a proud part of our heritage. They remind us of a time when hard work and dedication to duty by just a few rugged individuals could protect the lives of thousands who sailed past these shining beacons of hope, trust and security.

It is no surprise that the keepers who lived and worked at New England's lighthouses have become legends. Through raging storms and bitter cold they kept the lights burning. Facing danger and loneliness they kept the fog signals working. Their own survival at these remote outposts depended upon their ability to make good quick judgments and to display great courage and strength. Although these gallant souls faced many hardships, their lives were rich and rewarding as every new adventure challenged them to respond. They enjoyed a feeling of peace and satisfaction that made their lives worthwhile.

Time and climate have taken their toll on the New England lighthouses and the keeper's way of life has vanished into the past. The empty solitary structures, many now with rusting metal, evoke images of the spirits of those keepers who dedicated their lives to the beloved stations they called home. It is not difficult to imagine that even death could not stop their relentless devotion to duty. Perhaps their spirits are still wandering around the cold damp towers, climbing the stairs to the lantern rooms and checking the lights one more time. Keepers have become a piece of the lighthouse legend, a shining part of a proud New England legacy.

Boon Island

Boon Island Lighthouse rises up from a dangerous eight hundred foot ledge located six and one-half miles off the coast of York, Maine. Its one hundred and thirty-three foot gray granite tower is one of the most isolated stations on the Maine coast. Winter storms rock this island as tons of seawater throw enormous boulders from end to end, striking fear into the hearts of veteran lighthouse keepers. Only the tower and a generator house remain standing on the island today.

A TRIBUTE TO THE LEGENDARY KEEPERS

Lighthouse keeping was a lonely, almost desolate occupation. Because the stations were used to identify potential hazards, many were built on high headlands and outcroppings along remote areas of the coast. Some were located on small rocky islands to mark exposed ledges. Keepers sometimes felt abandoned at these isolated sites when extended periods of rough weather prevented them from leaving the lighthouse for weeks at a time. With no deliveries of mail and supplies, they soon learned to become independent in order to survive. There was a lot to do however, and they were not disheartened by their plight. Keeping the beacon lit and the fog signal sounding required both mental and physical endurance. The keepers and their families were up to the challenge and took great pride in their work.

Maintaining a lighthouse demanded responsibility and required a great deal of effort. All of the mechanical equipment had to operate in first class condition. If something broke down or was damaged, it had to be repaired immediately. This not only included the intricate working parts of the light itself, but the fog signal; the donkey motor that hauled the boat; the heating units in the house; the cables, ropes and hawsers; leaky roofs; peeling paint - the list goes on and on. Some of the work was difficult or complex but a lot of it was mundane – like polishing brass. There was brass everywhere at the station: the reflectors and fixtures in the light room; oil containers; pumps; dust pans; even brass coal hods. All of the brass that was exposed to the salt air needed regular scrubbing and shining.

The station buildings, continuously battered by the sea and wind, required constant scraping, puttying and painting. The tall light tower could be forty or fifty feet around and whitewashing this massive structure was tricky and dangerous. The job required two men, one to raise and lower lines fastened to a basket, and the other in the basket to apply the whitewash. Because the wash contained a caustic lime, the keepers had to wait for a calm sunny day - a light northwest wind would dry the wash hard and fast. They started at sunrise and hoped to finish by sunset.

Painting the black roof over the lantern room at the top of the tower was an even more perilous job. The one hundred foot tall tower might be perched on a ledge another sixty feet above the sharp rocks below. Taking on the role of a steeplejack, the keeper threw a thick rope up over the metal roof and secured it around the outside edge of the crowning black ball cap. He scaled the pinnacle and painted with one hand while he guided himself along the rope with the other. One careless misstep and he would fall. Everyone at the station was relieved when this job was completed and the keeper was safely back on the ground.

Storms created a great deal of the workload at the station. Although the keepers could often read the conditions of the sea and sky, they rarely predicted the actual severity of an approaching storm so they always prepared for the worst. When it looked like a storm was brewing, most keepers sent their families to shore. The anxiety was enormous. The fury of the ocean was measured in tons of weight. Under the right conditions (or in this case the wrong conditions) the turbulent sea could lift rocks weighing several tons and throw them violently against the house or tower, smashing the walls. Every loose item on the island could be washed away. The keepers scrambled to secure all of the equipment and gear, then they bolted and shuttered the windows and doors of the outbuildings.

Because the keepers risked being washed out to sea during the storm if they walked anywhere in the yard, they secured guide ropes between the buildings. Great combers struck with fury. The house and tower could shake from the pounding waves for several days and nights. As ice built up on the lantern room glass, as the wind gusted through the tower, the keepers had to keep their signals working, for now they were most needed by the unfortunate mariners who were at sea during the storm. Throughout the tempest the keepers maintained a constant vigil for any sign of distress along the shore. They were ready to initiate an immediate rescue if a ship was blown off course and grounded on the rocks below.

The work continued long after the storm passed, as the family cleaned up the station and restored it to its original condition. Damage might include sand and seaweed all over the grounds and throughout the house; chimneys filled with debris; shingles torn off the roof and leaks everywhere; clapboards ripped from the side of the residence and the outbuildings; the boathouse and ramp destroyed; equipment damaged and in need of repair. It could take months of hard labor to put the station back into working order.

The cold winter season by itself created more work for the keepers. A pleasant half hour row from the lighthouse to the mainland in the summer months could be a dangerous two or three hour ordeal in the winter. When the air is colder than the water, a thick mist of sea vapor, about six to ten feet high, forms along the surface of the ocean and cuts the visibility to nearly zero. Ice flows create hazards as large chunks of ice moving with the tidal current bounce off the sides of the boat. On windy days extra precaution had to be taken to prevent frostbite. The keepers heated bricks in the oven the night before a journey, wrapped them in blankets the next morning and then loaded them into the dory, hoping they might provide some heat for the trip.

Landing the boat in winter was also more difficult, especially during a snowstorm. The keeper needed to see the run of the surf in order to make a safe landing. He would lay off the slip until the right wave came along, then pull on the oars and ride the wave in - surfboard style. If his timing was off he could be slammed onto the rocks or capsized by the heavy surf and end up in the frigid water. Once he landed safely, he still had to make his way carefully along the slippery ice covered rocks and ramps to get back to the lighthouse.

No matter what the circumstances were around them, the keepers' first responsibility was to keep their light burning and their signal sounding. When it was necessary, they were always able to display the strength, endurance and courage needed to perform their duty. Future generations will find their stories inspiring. One person who exemplifies these inspiring qualities is Connie Small, a lighthouse keeper's wife.

CONNIE SMALL - A Legend in Her Time

Connie was born June 4, 1901 and her entire life was filled with experiences associated with the sea. Her grandfather was a sea captain, her uncle a shipmaster and lighthouse keeper. Her dad was the third man in charge of the crew at Quoddy Head Life-Saving Station and her sister was married to a lighthouse keeper. At the age of nineteen, Connie married Elson Small, a man who had sailed since he was fourteen years old and had salt in his veins. From 1920 to 1948 they were lighthouse keepers at many lighthouses along the New England coast. As of January 1998 (the time of this writing), at the age of ninety-six, Connie has just completed her five hundred and twenty-first lecture about lighthouses and their impact on her life. When the author interviewed Connie, she enjoyed reminiscing about her family and some of her experiences and adventures as a lighthouse keeper's wife.

Elson worked for both the United States Lighthouse Service and the United States Coast Guard. Connie was proud to have been associated with both agencies. The Lighthouse Service was established under the administration of President George Washington. The families working for the commissioners of lighthouses were loyal, dedicated, concerned with each other's needs, and they endured many hardships. They were the true guardians of the coast. When the Coast Guard took the agency over in 1939, Connie witnessed many fast-moving technological changes including the conversion of the lighthouses to electricity. Her pride in and dedication to the Coast Guard did not waiver. She has some rich memories about her lighthouse service as a keeper's wife in both branches of government.

West Quoddy Head Light

The tower's red and white horizontal stripes are unique for Maine lighthouses. The light was rebuilt in 1858 and the station has undergone only a few minor changes since that time.

Connie's recollection of her experiences begin a few years before her marriage to Elson who was sailing with the Merchant Fleet during World War I. Connie was helping her dad, Ira Scovill, at the U.S. Life-Saving Station at Quoddy Head in Lubec, Maine. When a ship foundered, the life-saving crew rushed into action. They quickly pulled a small cannon to the site of the wreck. Connie scurried along with them, carrying a brass powder tin which was used to ignite the cannon. The rescuers wasted no time in firing some lines over to the wreck and a breeches buoy was soon attached to the ropes. A type of harness with a pair of short legged breeches hanging from it, the breeches buoy was pulled over to the ship. One by one, the crew and passengers would climb into the breeches and be pulled safely to shore by the life-saving crew. These rescues usually occurred during severe weather and there was little time for error because the ships could be broken up or swamped at any time. The strength and endurance of the ship's crew and the life-saving men were extremely important. The rescuers also had to be skilled in the art of launching surfboats in all kinds of heavy seas. It was a rough job for tough men. Fighting against all odds and challenging the great power of the sea, life-saving men saved many people from death and disaster. After the crew and passengers had been rescued, they would try to save the cargo and the vessel itself.

United States Coast Guard Photo

A Breeches Bouy Rescue Underway

Ira Scovill was a rugged fearless individual, 5 feet 10 1/2 inches tall. He had broad shoulders and was as strong as an ox. During World War I he trained recruits in the art of lifesaving. Part of the recruit training was sending men out on patrol to "carry out the watch." He trained the men to stay on the water's edge, watch for signals, listen for the sound of a distress call, and always keep a sharp lookout for any unusual lights. Patrolling was not a pleasant duty, especially when the weather was foul, but despite the wind, rain, cold or ice, the men stood their watch and remained vigilant.

One evening Ira was faced with a dilemma he had never encountered before. The men on watch at Quoddy Head had sighted a shadowy elusive figure that seemed to follow them as they patrolled. The ghastly apparition was pale, unearthly and unnatural. Perhaps this was the spirit of a dead keeper from the lighthouse. It moved with the men and seemed to mimic them. The recruits were agitated and asked Ira if the apparition could cause them harm. They did not want to go out on watch. Ira took his job seriously, and believed that one should carry out his duty no matter what dangers lay ahead. He also did not believe in ghosts. He chided the recruits for their foolishness and, being the strong leader that he was, turned up his jacket collar and took off on the watch by himself.

As he walked along the steep foggy path toward the lighthouse, lo and behold, he encountered some movement similar to what the men had described. Something appeared to be coming out of the woods. The ghostly figure stayed a short distance away but it followed every one of Ira's moves. Ira was bemused and beginning to think that the recruits were not foolish after all. He

United States Coast Guard Photo

An Unidentified Life Saving Crew In Storm Gear

13

felt obliged to report the situation but he was not about to run away. He tried to attack the ghost but the spirit disappeared into the woods. Ira tried to catch his breath; he was chilled to the bone by the bitter cold fog. The animated figure of the ghost appeared again.

"Preposterous! Ridiculous!" Ira shouted, more to himself than to the apparition.

The spirit was mocking him. Ira raised his lantern in a sweeping circle and the ghost appeared to do the same thing. Ira lunged at the ghost and it disappeared. Then he stepped back and the figure came toward him again. He raised his lantern and the spirit made the same motion with its arm.

"Good grief!" Ira exclaimed, "The ghost is my shadow!"

The mystery was solved. The strange figure that had appeared was nothing more than the shadow of the person on the path, cast by the lighthouse beacon and reflected on the heavy water droplets of the thick fog. Ira gave the recruits a stern lecture about danger and duty and the regular watches continued on schedule. The phantom ghost at Quoddy Head would terrorize no more.

Lighthouses have been built in many different shapes and configurations. The first light that Elson Small was assigned to was Lubec Channel Light at Lubec, Maine. This was a round structure referred to as a "spark plug" lighthouse. New England has several of these light stations. Built on pilings in the middle of a river or harbor, these formidable structures seem to pop up out of the water. Most round lighthouses were "stag stations" manned by two or more men who split the duty time. Stag stations were not built with family quarters in mind.

In the middle and late 1800's the sardine canning industry was flourishing along the shores of Lubec. Large seiners were bringing in tons of fish. The ship captains were having a difficult time navigating the St. Croix River and its dangerous channel. A light station was needed to properly mark the area and Lubec Channel Light was built and first lit in 1890. Rising fifty-three feet above the surface, it sits on a concrete and cast iron foundation, or caisson, and is entirely surrounded by water. The tower was painted white. The interior shell of the round structure was lined with brick.

Living in a partially submerged round tower was a unique experience. The main platform tower door was the entrance to

United States Coast Guard Photo

Lubec Channel Light
A "spark plug" light, Lubec Channel Light was built in 1890.

the living quarters. A stove, sink, bookcase, rocking chair, couch, table and chairs were arranged neatly in the room. The brick walls were painted white, the windows were square and the view was magnificent. Cleaning was made easy by the fact that there were no corners. Two spiral stairways were attached to the wall, one going up to the second level bedroom and the other going down to the circular basement. Since these were stag stations they were very sparsely furnished. A bed, commode and single chair were the only furnishings in the bedroom. There were five deck levels in the tower - the third level was another bedroom, the watch room was on the fourth level, and the lantern room was the fifth level.

Sleeping in the tower was not easy, especially for a newcomer. Strange noises echoed through the different levels. The wind blew around the structure on all sides. The sound from waves crashing against the foundation was amplified in the basement. It took a long time for the keepers to get used to the building and recognize its normal strange sounds.

At one time the light was run by kerosene. When lit, the cotton wick provided the light behind the lens. It had to be perfectly trimmed, with no rough ends or frays, or it would cause a smoke-up when it burned and create an awful mess. The smoke would stick like grease on the lens, the lantern windows and the brass fixtures in the room. Cleaning up the residue required many hours of tough scrubbing and polishing.

Keepers were constantly cleaning both the inside and outside glass of the lens room so the beacon would shine clear, steady and bright. Climbing through a small metal door, they could access the steel platform that surrounded the outside of the lens room. This could be pleasant duty on a warm summer day but during an icy winter storm it could become deadly. On many mornings the keepers would have to clean feathers and bird debris from the lantern windows because the light would attract flocks of ducks and geese that crashed into the glass and died. Cleaning this mess was another unpleasant task, but the fresh killed birds scattered about the platform provided a steady supply of fresh game birds for the evening meal.

16

Because round lighthouses were stag stations, the bathroom facilities were very crude. A bathroom was an open outhouse located on a small deck that extended out over the ocean below. The tiny shed was located on the first outer deck platform. If "mother nature" called during a raging blizzard, the keepers held on for dear life.

Another interesting (and perhaps disquieting) area of the lighthouse was the basement where the coal and supplies were kept. The keepers were always aware of the fact that they were under the water level when they entered the basement - the sound of the sea rushing past the walls was deafening. When the strong current pushed a log or piece of wood into the structure, the noise was like a cannon firing, rattling the keepers nerves. They looked at the iron plates and rivets on the wall and hoped that the seams held fast and that nothing let go. Rain water collected by gutters on the roof was used for drinking and cleaning at the station. A system of pipes fed into storage cisterns that were located under the basement floor and were accessible through manhole covers. Without rain there was no fresh water.

The tide in the bay where Lubec Channel Light sits has a swift current with about a twenty-eight foot rise and fall. Some of the keepers assigned to the station have been lost to the sea. One young substitute keeper, an excellent artist, loved his duty at the light because it gave him a chance to work on his oil paintings. He had just completed a shift for the full-time keeper and was getting ready to leave the tower. As he descended the ladder with a canvas painting tucked under one arm, he slipped and fell to his death. His body was recovered two days later about three miles downstream from the light station. Another keeper died when he was asphyxiated by fumes from the coal burner.

When keepers approached the lighthouse they would maneuver their dory or boat to a position just beneath an outside ladder. The skipper had to be an excellent navigator to keep the boat in place against the fast tidal current because the station had no dock. The visitors would have to grab hold of the rungs on the suspended ladder and climb up the outside of the tower to the entrance. When Elson was assigned to the light Connie was allowed to visit the stag station. On her first trip she spotted the ladder and knowing she would have to climb it, she was almost overwhelmed by panic. There were thirty rungs up to the first small iron platform and then fifteen more up another ladder to the main deck. Scaling the ladders seemed endless and treacherous and Connie knew that if her hand or foot slipped from the iron bar she would fall into the rushing waters below. As she started to climb, fear and anxiety took over her body and she did not want to continue. Elson was climbing behind her and he calmly said, "Connie, look up and never look down."

She reached the first platform and then she did look down. Once again she was nervous that she would not be able to make it up the next ladder. She looked up again and completed the climb. She was a courageous woman and conquered her fears. After Elson reached the main platform, he quickly secured the lines he had tied to both ends of the boat so he could haul it up and suspend it from the side of the tower to keep it safely above the water.

On another visit to the light the bottom part of the ladder had rusted off. At high tide the ladder could still be reached from the boat and Connie was able to climb up to the station without any problems. When she was ready to leave however, the tide was low and there was a considerable drop from the bottom of the ladder into the boat. Elson pulled the boat up onto the platform, she climbed in, and he slowly lowered it down to the sea below. Since he was manning the light alone, he had to let one end of the boat down at a time. Connie was glad that the lines didn't slip because she would have gone headfirst into the surging sea. Elson was a skilled seaman and everything turned out fine. Elson dropped down into the boat and rowed her back to the mainland three quarters of a mile away. Captain Small was stationed at Lubec Channel Light for two years. Connie has lived her entire life with the philosophy she adopted on her first visit to the lighthouse - she always looks up and never looks down. Her positive attitude, logic and basic truths have given her a wisdom that has served her well.

Elson and Connie's next assignment was at Avery Rock, located at the southern end of Machias Bay. Built in 1875, approximately three miles out to sea, it was situated on a very open and exposed location. The rocky ledge was a navigational hazard. It was so small that the lighthouse was designed to have the beacon on top of the main house in order to conserve space. The seas in this area are furious. During storms, tons of water would bury the house and tower. When a storm threatened, Connie and Elson had to close the three inch thick shutters on the home's windows to keep the glass from being taken out. An attempt was made to divert some of the ocean by erecting a barrier just down from the main house. The bulkhead looked like a snow plow with a "V" shape which would split the surf. It washed away many times over the four years that the Smalls lived on this barren rock.

United States Coast Guard Photo

Avery Rock Light
Located on a tiny island in Machias Bay, this light was constructed in 1875. This was the second assignment for Elson and Connie Small.

Each and every day the Avery Rock beacon was lit precisely at sunset. The process involved the use of wood alcohol as a starter fuel which heated up the mantle until it was white hot. At exactly the right moment, Elson turned on the kerosene, the fire would vaporize and the main light was lit. Because supplies on the island were limited, not a drop of fuel or oil could be wasted. The gears and mechanisms that rotated the light were oiled every few days with special machine oil kept in a small bottle one half inch high and one inch around. Captain Small used the end of a feather to get the one tiny drop needed to keep the gears free. This little bottle contained the entire year's supply of oil needed for this important job. Connie and Elson could tell if the light was functioning properly just by listening to the sounds it made as the beacon rotated. It was like the rhythmical humming of a sewing machine, and any variation meant that something was out of order.

Two years after Connie and Elson had left the island, on January 28, 1928 one of the worst storms ever recorded passed over the island. The waves were intense; the entire sea was a mass of turbulence. The keeper in charge at the time, keeper E.A. Pettigrew, sincerely believed that the entire property would be destroyed. For some reason his common sense, instinct or good judgment caused him to open all of the windows and doors in the lighthouse and to cut a hole in the dining room floor. With his wife and mother-in-law in tow, he climbed behind the station's cast iron stove and held on for dear life. The mighty Atlantic roared through the house, destroying their furniture and belongings but the structure held and their lives were spared. This was a harrowing experience.

The storms could cut the lighthouse off from communication and supplies for long periods of time, and the keeper had to be careful not to let his stocks run too low. When weather permitted, Captain Small rowed over to the mainland for supplies. If foul weather set in while he was on shore and he couldn't get back to the station, Connie was in charge. It was now her responsibility to make sure that the beacon was lit and that the fog signal sounded. If anything malfunctioned she had to fix it at once. Connie knew almost as much about the light station as Elson, having worked dauntlessly by his side.

One of Connie's more trying times occurred when Elson was sick and slipped into a coma. He had a very high fever. The weather was too rough for her to get help and for twelve days she kept the station running by herself while she also tried to nurse her husband back to health. She felt incredibly isolated. Connie said that around the fourth day she thought that she had lost Elson. She took his pulse and couldn't get a reading. She had to light the beacon and crank up the fog bell so she left his still body and fulfilled her obligations. Feeling terribly alone, she said a prayer.

At this point she felt that a Guardian Angel came into her life. After her duties as keeper were completed, she returned to Elson's room and looked at him lovingly. She felt helpless and wondered what she should do. In the next moment she heard his faint voice asking her for some cornmeal. She fed him tiny portions and over the next week he slowly gained back his strength. Her prayers had been answered. Despite her feelings of intense loneliness, Connie had summoned her inner strength and confidence and she learned firsthand the importance of self-reliance at the lighthouse. She did what she had to do.

Most of her time was spent completing mundane tasks. It was her responsibility to keep the station clean and polished. Inspections were stern, rigorous and unannounced - just a spot of dust over a door jam could be written up – but if the station passed they received a star. Elson and Connie took pride in keeping their station spotless and they received many citations and stars. She also tended the garden, growing vegetables to eat and preserve. Keepers received a small salary and the vegetables helped stretch the station budget. The wives were expected to carry out their duties without pay. Occasionally Elson would catch lobsters and sell them on the mainland for some extra funds.

In 1926 the Smalls were transferred to Seguin Light Station, one of the oldest stations on the coast of Maine. It was established under President George Washington's administration in 1795. They would be stationed there for the next four years. Because of the heavy boat traffic on the Kennebec and Sheepscott

Rivers, Seguin was an important station. The island is one of the highest on the coast. Its one hundred and thirty-three foot elevation provided a great vantage point for a lighthouse, but it presented a challenge to get supplies up to the buildings. A small rail system was built from the beach to the top of the island. Supplies were loaded into a trolley car at the bottom of the hill and then a hoisting apparatus called a donkey motor would haul the tram up to the top. The keepers and guests walked up a steep quarter mile ramp next to the track.

Seguin Island Light Station
This station is located on a high point of land on a small island and is one of the foggiest locations along the Maine coast.

When the Smalls moved to Seguin the island was assigned three keepers. Elson was first in charge. The island had two homes, a single family for the main keeper and a duplex for the other two keepers' families. Seguin has the reputation of being at the foggiest location in Maine and the powerful foghorn blasts an average of one hundred and twenty days a year. The main keeper's house was just north of the powerful foghorn and Connie was thankful that the second keeper in charge had been living in that house with his family. She did not ask him to move. When the foghorn was activated, the residents could not hear each other speak and they learned to stop talking during the blasts. Connie remembers feeling the strong vibrations in the windows. It has been said that close flying sea gulls have been knocked right out of the air by the powerful signal.

Life on Seguin was active and with two other families stationed there with about ten children, it certainly was not lonely. Connie's duties were the same as at the other stations but she also became a Sunday school teacher, a babysitter, and she helped some of the children with their lessons. Children between the ages of four and eighteen were taught reading, writing and ciphering (arithmetic). The kids all had chores to do which also provided some of their education. Maps, globes and books were scarce but nautical maps were always on hand. A child might learn her ABC's or his prayers through the New England Primer. They learned math from a "copybook" – a blank book into which they would copy math problems from the teacher's book, thus creating a math textbook at their own level. An example of a good math question might be, "If two men can catch fifteen fish in one and one half hours, how many men will it take to catch three hundred fish in three hours?"

One of the primary skills the children learned was proper handwriting. They practiced their penmanship for many hours with pens made from feathers. Good manners were also taught. Rules of behavior were very important and the children were expected to be well behaved. Families might use a birch rod or strap as an integral part of their children's education. In the later years the school kids were sent to the mainland for their studies. On Sunday the children attended Sunday school taught by the keepers' wives right on the island.

Another unique aspect to living on an island was that uninvited strangers often dropped by to check out the lighthouse. One the funniest stories Connie tells, which she writes about in her book "The Lighthouse Keeper's Wife" published by the University of Maine Press, is about a visit from a monkey. Connie was up at sunrise on a beautiful day. She finished her chores early and decided to go blueberry picking with her friends who kept the light on Perkins Island. She climbed down the quarter mile ramp, launched the boat and headed toward Georgetown, about four and a half miles away. She picked about a bushel of the most perfect blueberries - large, ripe and juicy. She cruised home, docked the boat, and carried her blueberries up to the house. The afternoon sun was bright and warm; she would winnow the berries (remove the leaves and stems} in the backyard. She went into the kitchen to get the canning supplies ready. The berries would be a delicious treat in the spring when the island's food supply ran low. Suddenly she heard a clamor on the lawn and wondered what the commotion was. She ran out on the porch and saw a monkey in the blueberry basket, chewing and spitting berries in all directions. "A monkey on Seguin Island?" she thought. "Impossible!"

Like many other summer tourists, it seems a yachtsman passing in his boat wanted to get a closer look at the lighthouse. Unlike the others, this tourist had a pet monkey with him. After he docked he took the monkey on shore and climbed up to the buildings. The monkey immediately spotted the blueberries, broke free, and had a picnic. Connie was upset. Her day's efforts were wasted and there would be no blueberries next spring for the keepers. None of this seemed to bother the uninvited guests who were promptly asked to leave the island.

Seguin is one of the several Maine lighthouses that have a reputation of being haunted. Over the years several unusual incidents have occurred on the island that could be classified as ghostly phenomena. Connie Small, like her dad, does not believe in ghosts but she did have one experience on the island for which she has no rational explanation.

The bright crisp day started off normally. The Smalls got up at sunrise and Elson started his work while Connie prepared breakfast - biscuits, cereal, bacon, and hot tea.. They ate together and talked for a few moments before he left to go down to the generator house to check on some equipment. Connie was cleaning up the kitchen when she heard the door open and close. She called

Elson's name but didn't receive an answer. She entered the living room and was startled to see a man with red curly hair standing in the hall. He had a fair complexion and large blue eyes. He was shivering and shaking and appeared very cold. With a discernable brogue, he asked her if he could lie down next to the warm kitchen stove. Connie consented and he walked into the kitchen, dropped to his hands and knees, crawled behind the oven, stretched out and fell asleep. She watched him as she puttered around the living room. About an hour later he crawled out, stood up and thanked her. She offered him some food but he refused with another polite thank you. He proceeded to the door, turned, and with a beautiful brogue, gave her an Irish blessing.

Connie was impressed by this clean, well mannered seaman and she was concerned that he might have needed more help. She alerted Elson and the other keepers who searched the island, but no tracks or trace of the man were found and there was no boat near the landing. The man had disappeared as fast and mysteriously as he had appeared. Could he have been an apparition of one of the many shipwrecked sailors who have lost their lives off of Seguin? No one will ever know.

In 1930 Connie and Elson were transferred from Seguin to Saint Croix River Light Station (Dochet Island) on the border between Maine and New Brunswick, Canada. When she arrived on the island, she wrote the following words:

Today I stand by the window and view my new home. Looking across the river a half mile away I see the church with its doors flung wide, its bell chiming "Oh come, come, to the little church" and I watch its members enter. The only thing familiar is the church bell call, for I am just like a flower suddenly transplanted into a new home and location.

I vision the people taking their seats, the organist beginning the prelude sending the sacred tones of the organ into every crevice and corner of both church and occupant, bringing spontaneous joy into their hearts, expressing itself in shine of eyes and smile of lips. A sadness possesses me for though I am there in Spirit my body is absent and I turn away feeling alone in my island home, a stranger in a strange land. But immediately one who forsakes us not is beside me, my heart quickens, joy wells up within me, and with confidence I say, "My company is legion," for has He not said, "I will send my angels to watch over you."

Oil Painting by Ron Goyette

The door opens and my husband enters followed by our pet cat and life begins again; this life that is of the earth, earthy. My husband speaks, "It's no use, the stern post in the dinghy is rotten beyond repair; I've sawed the whole end out and boarded it up square. Sure will be a funny looking dinghy but it will have to do until we can find one. I was talking to a man in the Post Office yesterday and he says that a couple of brothers up river about a couple of miles build them for a hundred dollars each. That is a lot of money just now so I think I'll get some lumber and try to build one for myself. Asa Pede says he will help me. He builds fine boats and I can trade in my fishing trawl as he has been trying to get one."

"When you put your power boat on the bank for winter, how will we get to the mainland?" I said. "We'll have to use this row boat," he answered, "and in the spring we'll buy an outboard motor."

Even this break into ordinary things could not console me so I turned to my husband saying, "I've felt lonesome today, hearing the church bell I guess, and seeing the people going to worship; all strangers; makes me feel alone, sort of apart from the world. Do you suppose I could go over some day?"

"It will not be possible this fall or winter but perhaps by spring you will be acquainted and will not feel so lonely," he said. "Why don't you put on your coat and come to the beach with me, it's nice down there in the sun." He waited affectionately for me to get ready.

We ventured out into the crisp, breezy afternoon with its smell of frost and with a whistle to Topsy, our kitty who follows us around like a puppy, we started down the path to the beach. Halfway down we passed through the pasture gate and were joined by the other member of our family, Blossom the cow.

Winter was beginning to throw her blanket over the trees and nature was about to take its long winter nap. It brought to our minds our early settling forefathers who settled here long long ago, one hundred and twenty of them, fortifying themselves against the Indians, enduring one of the hardest winters in history. Our island home here consists of about five acres of sandy loom sloping from a barren high bank on the south to a wooded point on the north. On this south end where we were now were several sandy beaches spreading their light gray arms around two little nubbles separated by sandy bars.

The blue of the river was being whipped into white scallops to the north and east, sparkling like diamonds in the bright sunlight. The slop, slop of the tiny waves on the beach at my feet held my gaze for a moment as I thought, how angry the river yet here in this little sheltered cove only tiny ripples were occasionally being breathed across its placid surface as a sudden gust of wind swept down over the bank above us. The sea gull with its gray beak, its white lined wings and breast was soaring

27

overhead rising high then swooping low at the prospect of food Now and then a sandpiper runs along the edge of the water, its tiny legs moving so fast they are just a blur, their long bills incessantly pecking for food, its peep, peep at a fat juicy morsel. I speak severely to my cat who tries to catch them and she thrashes her tail from side to side, angry because I have spoiled her hunt.

"Do you think that you ought to work like this today?" I said as I turned to my husband who is busy getting what used to be a very nice double end dinghy tight enough to float, and I dropped down beside him taking up bits of lead and fitting it into the seams. He looked up at me over the top of his glasses and we both laughed knowing that being idle is just one adventure which is irksome to both. So to justify my act yet longing to help, I say, "Spiritually we worship, materially we exist." To exist on an island a boat is necessary and a leaky boat is like a drowning soul, so the repair went steadily on until the sun hid itself behind a cloud withdrawing its warming companionship. We shiver and my husband collects his tools. It's too cold now to continue.

Topsy sprints up the bank, looking back with the expression of don't you wish you were as agile as I? Blossom undisturbed by feline fleetness lumbers along behind, now and then running her rough tongue over my husband's back until he has to shoo her away. Reaching the top of the bank we bend into the wind which is not only brisk now but cold, stinging our eyes and causing the tears to flow down over our cheeks. My husband says, "I'll race you to the gate," and I start a race lost from the beginning but successful in warming the body and promoting comradeship.

We enter our home and I go to the window to look out over the water at the little church. Its bell is still, the doors closed, the worshipers departed It's not friendly anymore; there is no calling spirit across the water. I turn to find my husband standing behind me and as I am enfolded in his embrace I am no more lonely or alone, I am rich in possession, and God is with us all.

"A Page From Life," Sept. 1930, Constance Small

St. Croix River Light Station was built in 1857 on a very historical island. In 1604-1605 this island was used by Samuel Champlain as a base when he discovered and charted the northeast coast. The island marks the entrance to the Saint Croix River which is part of the border between the United States and Canada. The entire lighthouse complex was burned down in 1976 by a group of youngsters seeking shelter on the island. They started a fire for warmth in the main house, which quickly got out of control, and high winds spread the flames to all of the buildings at the station.

United States Coast Guard Photo

St. Croix River Light

When Connie and Elson moved to the island the keeper's residence looked like a one-room schoolhouse or an old New England meeting house; the light tower sat on top of the roof like a bell tower or steeple. The Smalls spent sixteen happy years on this island. Because of its close proximity to the mainland, they were able to get a truck over to the island which was a big help to them when they planted the fertile part of the land. They also had their own cow so fresh milk was always available. Even Connie's fifteen pound cat enjoyed the surroundings. Life on Saint Croix River Light Station was gratifying. Farming, fishing, chores, repairs, cooking, cleaning, and entertaining their many guests kept them busy. During their stay here they felt that this lighthouse was truly their home.

In 1946 Elson was transferred again, this time to the Portsmouth Harbor Light Station located at Fort Point in New Castle, New Hampshire. Portsmouth Light was one of the original twelve colonial lighthouses built before the American Revolution that were ceded to the new United States. Four months before the revolution, a group of New Hampshire Minute Men disarmed a company of British Regulars at this site, taking their guns and cannon. These were later used against the British at the Battle of Bunker Hill. In 1784 Captain Titus Salter became the keeper at this historic site, and oversaw the construction of a permanent light tower which was personally inspected by President George Washington in 1789. Connie and Elson were again moving to a place with lots of history.

In 1872 a wood frame keeper's house had been built at the station and in 1877 a new tower was erected. The light station was on the mainland so Connie's life was much simpler. Groceries, supplies and all necessities were driven right up to the front door. This was also the first time that Connie would live with electricity, a washing machine, a telephone and a refrigerator. She could even drive into town and buy some bakery goods!

One of the major responsibilities at this station was to make sure that the weather flags were properly hoisted. Portsmouth Harbor was an extremely busy port and captains watched for these flags which signaled approaching storms, hurricanes, gales and any other conditions that could be hazardous to the mariners.

In 1948 Connie and Elson left Portsmouth, their last station. As lighthouse keepers they had lived a life few people would ever experience. With the end of the manned lighthouse era, only a handful of people will ever be able to experience that way of life. Through her teaching, writing and lectures to all age groups, Connie has touched the lives of thousands of people and allowed them to see a part of history that has disappeared. Her book "The Lighthouse Keeper's Wife" (University of Maine Press 1986) is well worth reading. Elson passed away in 1960. As of the writing of this book (January 1998) Connie is ninety-six years old and still going strong. Her enthusiasm for life and her positive attitude is contagious.

KEN BLACK, "MR. LIGHTHOUSE" - Another Legend

Ken Black, known locally as "Mr. Lighthouse," was born in 1923. He is seventy-five years young and over fifty of those years were spent either on the sea or working at lighthouses. Ken is the director and founder of "Maine's Lighthouse Museum," the Shore Village Museum in Rockland, Maine.

Ken Black

In September 1941, three months before Pearl Harbor, Ken enlisted in the United States Coast Guard. During the war he served on various ships and stations; he performed rescue operations, spent time on buoy tenders and worked on cargo ships in the Pacific. Soon after the war he commanded the Coast Guard Group at Quoddy Head, Maine and all of the light stations in that area were under his jurisdiction. When Ken retired after thirty-two years of active service, he was Chief Warrant Officer, W4, and held the distinction of being the Senior Warrant Officer in the entire United States Coast Guard.

I asked Ken to share some of his lighthouse experiences with me. His first comment was that life at a lighthouse could be very hard. Many tasks that seem routine on the mainland could present special challenges on an island station. One of the most difficult jobs was the delivery of oil and water to the station. A buoy tender loaded with the supplies cruised out to the island and everyone prayed for calm seas. The tender shot large lines attached to hoses over to the island. The keepers retrieved the lines and then dragged the heavy hoses through the surf and across the island to the tanks. The men were working on snaggy irregular rocks and the lines could get caught up in the uneven notches, requiring the keepers to carefully climb the slippery pinnacles to clear them. When the tanks were filled and the tender motored off the keepers breathed a collective sigh of relief.

Moose Peak Lighthouse near Jonesport, Maine had water cisterns that could only hold up to six thousand gallons of water. Built in 1827 under the presidency of John Quincy Adams, Moose Peak Light was located on Mistake Island. Two tiny faucets provided the only fresh water from the small cisterns in the duplex house. Commander Black wanted a larger and more accessible fresh water storage system installed for the men, so he took a visitor from the United States Public Health Service out to the island and complained that the men were all experiencing dental problems. When the official wanted to know why, Ken informed him that the men had to drink large quantities of soda pop because of the lack of water storage. Within a short time he had his large cisterns.

United States Coast Guard Photo

Moose Peak Lighthouse

The original station was established in 1827. The current tower, shown here, was built in 1851.

It was another perilous adventure when white gas had to be delivered to the station. Many lighthouses depended upon batteries for some of their power needs and the batteries were charged by a generator fueled by the gas. Some of the water pumps were also operated by gasoline. The gas was stored in drums that had to be transferred from the tenders to the island. Once again, the keepers had to negotiate the sharp shoreline with a great deal of caution as they maneuvered the gas drums into position on the island.

There was a great deal of tension and strain created by the weather at the station, and not just because of the damage and extra work involved. The keepers were totally dependent upon the ability of the tenders to get to the light; weather was a critical factor for the successful delivery of supplies to the island. Strict conservation measures had to be taken if supplies were running low and a period of bad weather was predicted. The keepers also watched the sea and sky carefully as the departure date for their scheduled shore leave approached. Bad weather could keep them on the island for extra days.

The average person takes good nutrition for granted, but eating properly and maintaining a balanced diet at a lighthouse could be a problem. When supplies were running low, food was rationed to make it last. It was not unusual for keepers to eat peanut butter sandwiches at breakfast, lunch and dinner for days at a time. Even when food was abundant the keepers did not always eat as they should. Some hated to cook, but others tried to stretch their budgets. Each month they were given a fixed amount of money to buy their groceries and any money they didn't spend they could keep. Some tried to live as frugally as possible, pinching pennies on their grocery list so they would have some extra cash when they went ashore. When Commander Black inspected the light stations, he occasionally found some of the men suffering from malnutrition. The well-being of the men was always his top priority and he would conduct a "freezer check" to make sure that the men were purchasing the right kinds of food and that they were using it. Ken said that at times it was like a game.

One thing the men did eat was fresh seafood. The local lobster men knew the keepers and sometimes left them part of their catch. The keepers fished off the rocks and could land some good-sized fish and they also used their dories around the island to fish and set their own lobster traps.

At times, lighthouse keepers had to be both imaginative and clever to solve some interesting problems that could occur in an island home. With the conversion from outhouses to indoor plumbing, sewer pipes had to be laid across the solid ledge for direct discharge into the sea below. The second tallest lighthouse in Maine, Petit Manan Light, stands one hundred nineteen feet high and one hundred twenty-three feet above the high water mark. There is not much slope from the complex to the ocean and it required a long sewer line, completely exposed above ground, running at a slight pitch out to the sea. In the summer this line worked perfectly but in winter it would always freeze and cause a severe backup into the house. The men devised and installed a

Petit Manan Light
The station was established in 1817. The current tower was built in 1855.

unit called a "sanitary Y" - a kind of junction halfway down the pipe. When the backup occurred, they burned old rubber tires at the junction to thaw the line. This sometimes created a small explosion from the buildup of sewer gasses, but the lines would be cleared! Life at the lighthouse was interesting, to say the least.

Libby Island Light, perched on a steep cliff at the southwestern end of the Libby Island group, marks the entrance to Machias Bay, Maine. The ledge below the structure drops down sharply about sixty feet to a patch of spiked rocks whose jagged irregular edges have been carved out by the ever flowing turbulent sea. When the outhouse at this station was converted to an inside toilet, the sewer line was dropped over the edge of the cliff into a gorge and the open end of the pipe was left hanging a few feet above the water line. This seemed like a good idea at the time but when the winds picked up, they blew up through the line and into the hopper. It was a rather startling experience until the keepers became accustomed to the loud noises coming from the toilet and it gave new meaning to the term "howling winds." Perhaps this is how some of the ghost stories originated at different lighthouses. Each lighthouse is exposed to its own strange sounds and active imaginations can be very creative.

United States Coast Guard Photo

Libby Island Light

36

On a more serious note, Libby Island Light Station has been the site of many disastrous shipwrecks. The main island is connected by a sand bar to the next island, but from the sea there appears to be an open passage between the two. Some captains have made the serious error of thinking they were going through a gut, only to be left high and dry on the sand bar. The *Caldonia* ran aground in 1878 during a violent storm and its captain and one seaman drowned. A short time later the bark *Fame* sank here with three crewmen lost out of fifteen. Captain McDonald and the surviving crew were saved by a boatswain chair manned by the lighthouse keepers. In 1892 Captain John Brown sailed the *Princeport* into a ferocious rain storm and miscalculated the gap. The lighthouse keepers saved the crew and captain who clung to a tiny piece of the bowsprit. In May of 1923 the three masted schooner *Lockhart* mysteriously grounded in perfect weather. The ship was lodged so securely that nothing could be done to lift it off the bar and it eventually broke up in the winter storms that followed. A total of thirty-five wrecks were reported between 1856 and 1902 with fifteen lives lost.

The keepers were not immune to dangers either. On June 18, 1918 Samuel Holbrook drowned off Libby Island while fishing in his small boat. A sea swell capsized his boat and Holbrook was lost. Commander Black lost one of his men out here in a similar accident. Leland Carter, a young man very well liked by the crew, decided to go duck hunting. He had spent the previous night working on a broken generator and did not get the machine up and running until dawn. After the long night, he decided to take the next day for some "R&R" and he rowed over to the next island to hunt. One of the other crew members looked out the window and saw Leland and his dog in the peapod, but a short time later the boat was sighted upside down. The crew quickly alerted the Coast Guard station at Cross Island for help and a thirty foot boat was dispatched immediately. Although the ocean was calm, the swells were large. When they reached the scene the men discovered the seaman and his dog floating in the water. Apparently Carter's jacket had filled with air and his head was pushed under the waves. The dog had hit his head on the sharp ledges. This was a tough loss for the commander and his men.

The peapod was the classic boat used to get on and off the islands. The fifteen foot wooden boat was rounded on the bottom and had a double end – the front and back were both pointed. The boat was rowed from a kneeling position. The skipper would row looking forward, so he could run with the tide and hope to hit the landing. Many light stations had two landings side-by-side. If the keeper missed one, he might hit the other. The sea is tricky and treacherous and if the peapod was turned around by the surf, it could be landed in either direction and no time was lost turning the boat. The Coast Guard built all of their small wooden boats at the boatyard in Curtis Bay, Maryland. Because of its sea battered rocky coastline, heavy surf and extreme tides, the Commanders were well aware of the difficult landings at the Maine stations. By 1956 Maine was the only area in which peapods were still being used, as their design was perfectly suited for these exposed locations.

Commander Black looked out for his people. He was committed to their safety and concerns and was always interested in any problems his crew or their families experienced. He did all in his power to make the lives of his charges rewarding and happy. His lighthouses were always safe and secure. A great leader must be concerned and involved, and Commander Black did his job well. He is carrying on that tradition of excellence through his civic devotion and expertise at the Shore Village Museum in Rockland, Maine.

WORLD WAR II

During World War II many light stations were refitted to serve a dual purpose. Lookout towers were constructed next to many of the signal towers and they were manned by men and women watching for German submarines, airplanes or suspicious activity. The watches were every four hours - four on and four off. The signal bulbs in the Fresnel lenses were also changed to a much lower wattage so the signal would not aid the German sub commanders looking for entrances to the ports and harbors.

The Coast Guard and the Coast Guard Auxiliary patrolled the shoreline twenty-four hours a day. Many large private homes, hotels, and guest houses with sweeping ocean views were taken over by the government and turned into military stations. A lot of folks were proud to let the service use their homes, as it was all part of the giant war effort. The converted buildings were used by the Coast Guard as bases from which the shore patrols could operate. The men, armed with rifles and sometimes accompanied by trained dogs, marched back and forth along the rocky shore, passing each other at regular intervals. The concerns were that

United States Coast Guard Photo
World War II Coast Guard Beach Patrol

German U boats would drop off saboteurs who would raise havoc in defense plants or try to poison reservoirs. Many patrols were sent on wild goose chases after seeing unexplained lights just off the coast because every call was checked.

Diesel engines could often be heard just offshore when the German submarines would surface to recharge their batteries. Many of them were chased back out to sea by local patrol boats.

In several cases, the subs were trapped and sunk when a destroyer reached the scene. Frank Philbrick of York Harbor, Maine chased a sub in his tiny unarmed patrol boat all the way from the Nubble Lighthouse out to Boon Island, a distance of eight miles. When he called for help, a destroyer was dispatched from the Portsmouth Naval Shipyard. It soon found the sub and sank it with several depth charges.

It was not uncommon for plaster walls to crack or pieces of ceiling to fall in seaside homes as a result of the reverberations from depth charges. The Coast Guard not only went after German subs, they also conducted many training exercises just a few miles from shore. Working with navy bombers, crews practiced runs against sea targets. The explosions were loud and coastal residents could hear and feel the tremble from the blasts.

The German boats were the most advanced submarines at the time. They were speedy, could recharge faster, and stay submerged longer than any other U boats afloat. Fifteen hundred American ships were sunk by these attackers. Following the allied invasion of France, a German U boat was captured and brought into the Portsmouth Naval Shipyard. Before the marines could march the crew of the sub from the pier to the naval prison across the base, precautions had to be taken to protect the prisoners. All of the employees at the shipyard were ordered to stay at their posts, the outside yards were cleared of all workers, and blackout curtains were drawn in the buildings so no one could see the Germans. It was feared that some workers would attack the German sailors but no incident occurred.

The Portsmouth Herald recently recounted an interesting story, as told by the captain of one of the cargo ships docked in the Portsmouth, New Hampshire harbor. The German captain told of an adventure he had on a much earlier visit to Portsmouth. He claimed that during the war, he slipped through the submarine nets and cleared the mines in the harbor. He told of how he followed a freighter in, close behind her stern, stayed around for a few days, looked over the Naval Base and then followed another ship out. When telling this story, he said he was much happier to be back on friendly terms and could only guess what would have happened to him and his crew if they had been caught.

When American ships were sunk just off the coast, little mention of it was made in the news. Folks who lived on the coastal plain always knew because oil slicks and coal dust would appear along the shore. Sometimes life buoys and debris would wash up on the beaches. The oil slicks killed the fish and waterfowl. It was certain that another United States Liberty Ship had gone down.

The end of the war marked the end of another chapter in lighthouse history. Once again the towers and the brave patriots who served in them provided a great service to the country.

United States Coast Guard Photo

Cape Neddick Light Station

Nubble Light, in York Beach, Maine, shown here with the observation tower that was erected during World War II. Note the pyramid shaped bell tower on the right which was removed in 1961 when the bell was replaced with a fog signal.

NUBBLE LIGHTHOUSE

The Cape Neddick Light Station, known as Nubble Light, has had its share of very unusual events. It was built in 1879 on a rockbound island off the tip of the Cape Neddick peninsula in York Beach, Maine. Although it is close to the mainland, it is a remote location. Under certain weather conditions it can be isolated for days at a time when passage through the narrow channel can be impossible due to rough seas.

United States Coast Guard Photo

Nubble Light

It is an impressive, almost stately structure. The six room victorian keeper's house has beautiful intricate gingerbread trim under the eves which highlights the roofline. The points of the roof line up with the compass points of north, south, east and west and many local airplane pilots check their direction when flying over the island. The round brick-lined tower is connected to the residence by a single story covered walkway. Before 1961 a pyramid structure was attached to the tower by another covered walkway. This building housed a twelve hundred pound bronze fog bell and the clocklike mechanism of weights which operated the striker. The keeper had to wind the weights by hand and if the mechanical striker failed, he would have to hit the bell with a hammer every fifteen seconds during foul weather until the equipment was repaired. The building was removed when the bell was replaced with an electric fog signal.

Many lighthouses used a system of gutters, pipes and storage cisterns to collect rain water for station use. The Nubble was no exception. Downspouts from the roof led to the cellar of the main house and emptied into a four thousand gallon tank. The first few minutes of rain carried with it all types of contamination including sea gull and other bird droppings. The keeper would place cups upside down over the downspouts to prevent the first rush of water from entering the cistern. When he felt the contamination was washed away, he removed the cups to allow the rest of the storm water to enter the tanks. In order to conserve the fresh water supply, baths were limited, especially during a dry season. Keepers had to constantly check the purity of the water and maintain the system by periodically scrubbing the tanks with bleach. The toilets were all salt water flushed.

THE NUBBLE LIGHT AREA & SHIPWRECKS

THE *ISADORE* - A Haunting Experience

Mysterious circumstances surrounded a shipwreck that occurred in the Nubble area in 1842, thirty-seven years before the Nubble Light station was built. On Thanksgiving night, the schooner *Isadore*, a three hundred and ninety-six ton barque, sailed out of Kennebunkport, Maine with a load of lumber destined for New Orleans. Just recently launched, the ship was named for the

43

infant daughter of the owner, Robert Smith, Jr. The captain, Leander Foss, was thirty-six years old.

Legend has it that one of the young crew members, Thomas King, refused to sail with the boat because he had a premonition that the ship was doomed. On the night of the ship's departure he hid in the woods despite the fact that he had already been paid a month's wages in advance. The captain was not about to sail without King and he ordered the crew to search the entire Kennebunkport area. They searched in vain, and the Captain had to set sail without the deserter.

A strong northeast wind was howling as Captain Foss charted a course out toward Boon Island. Nobody knows what happened that night; the captain may have beem attempting to head back to Kennebunkport when the vessel was driven aground. The next morning the *Isadore* was breaking up in Avery Cove in York. The waves were whipped up by the northeast winds and the bowsprit was totally underwater. Thirteen bodies had washed up on the shore. The rocks were littered with bits and pieces of the splintered ship. Dan Avery picked up a barrel of flour that had washed in from the wreck. News of the loss devastated the town of Kennebunkport since most of the crew members were from the town. Only Thomas King, who had experienced a mysterious premonition, was spared. When he returned to his home his family thought he was a ghost.

An interesting twist to the story concerns another crewmember, William Thompson (no relation to author). Apparently the boy was deciding whether he should become a farmer or choose a life at sea. His father had urged him to sail but his mother was totally opposed to the idea, feeling that her nineteen year old son was too young to make a life at sea. The father prevailed and the boy drowned in the *Isadore* disaster. For the next forty years the mother never spoke to her husband.

Since that Thanksgiving tragedy, many local fishermen have often reported seeing a ghostly image of a large ship that seems to sail on an endless course in the area. Perhaps this is the ghost of the *Isadore*.

Oil Painting by Ron Goyette

Sally Taylor, A Parting Farewell
Kennebunkport Harbor, Maine Circa 1842

THE ROBERT W

On January 12, 1923, Fairfield Moore, the keeper in charge of Nubble Light, witnessed the wreck of the *Robert W*. A severe storm had passed over the area blanketing the island and the town of York with snow. Captain Mitchell and his son Stanley had been caught in the storm on their way to Portsmouth Harbor when the forepeak halyard of the *Robert W* was carried away and the ship couldn't tack. They passed the Nubble and were driven ashore at Long Sands in York Beach. As the ship grounded, she listed on the starboard side, taking the full brunt of the heavy sea. Ice was building up on her fast because the temperature was about three degrees below zero. With a life preserver tied around each of their torsos, the Captain climbed one mast, Stanley the other, and they lashed themselves to the masts with heavy rope.

At about two o'clock, Howard Kelly, the second keeper on Boon Island Light who happened to be on shore leave in York, spotted the wreck. York resident Frank Philbrick had also seen the men in distress and with Kelly's help, he dragged a sixteen foot rowboat down from a beach cottage. The men launched the boat and tried to fight their way through the breaking surf to the site of the wreck but their attempts to reach the *Robert W* failed. The Portsmouth Navy Yard had been called to send a boat over from the Isles of Shoals with a breeches buoy (line and canvas breeches), but that boat was of no use because the heavy seas kept it well offshore. Finally at about ten o'clock that night, Frank and Howard made another attempt to launch the rescue dory further up the beach, figuring that this time the wind would blow them toward the ship. The strategy worked – they attached a line to the *Robert W* and the dory was secure.

Captain Mitchell cut his lifeline and slid to the deck, his hands and body badly frozen. Frank caught him around the legs and hauled him into the boat. Stanley fell from his mast and landed in the pounding sea. Frank immediately jumped into the ocean and grabbed the boy. The ice that had built up on Stanley's life preserver helped keep both men afloat. Frank claimed later that the water was a good deal warmer than the air, which was then five degrees below zero. A crew of volunteer rescuers who had gathered by the shore pulled the boat back to the beach. Frank and Stanley were still hanging onto the side of the dory when it safely reached the shore, and all of the men survived.

THE SPIRIT AT CAPE NEDDICK LIGHT STATION

Because of its rocky island setting just off the mainland, Nubble Light appears accessible yet remote. The one hundred nineteen year old buildings look like they have many stories to tell and the many visitors who look across from the shoreline often wonder if the lighthouse is haunted. Although there are no ghost stories to tell about this island, there seems to be some type of a good or happy spirit that seems to prevail in the area like an energy force of goodwill. Most of the keepers that have served at this light station have not wanted to leave when their duty was up and many asked for extensions. The reason they gave was that despite the hardships caused by living on an island, the lighthouse is a happy place to live and work.

Every year thousands of people drive for many miles to look at the lighthouse. They park their cars in the large parking lot at the end of the mainland and sit, meditate, and relax. Many speak of how much better they feel after spending time in the area. One woman tells of an incredible incident she experienced in her life during the spring of 1996. She was from a mid-Atlantic state. Her twenty-five year marriage seemed over, her life was in turmoil, and she was in a total state of confusion. She left her home, more than five hundred miles away from York, on a Monday evening at eight o'clock. Her goal was to drive somewhere, anywhere, to end her life. With no destination in mind and no particular plan, she started driving toward the northeast and drove aimlessly for about nine hours until she found herself along the rocky coast of Maine, a place she had never visited before.

Seeing a sign that read "Nubble Road" she turned and followed the narrow winding road out to the lighthouse. Her objective was to commit suicide. She sat looking at the lighthouse and was contemplating how to end her life when dawn broke over the horizon. It was a hazy morning and she could hear the soft, full tone of the foghorn while the red light from the beautiful glowing beacon (a light that never fails) reflected off the waves and shimmered on her car. A feeling of security came over her, a sense of stability, hope and trust, as though a spirit was with her in the car, guiding her toward wisdom and urging her to use good judgment. She knew that nobody was in the car but she was receiving a message that life can change for the better; that the rough spots can be smoothed out. A fresh ocean breeze brushed her face and her life came back together, her troubles passed. Inspired by her visit to the Nubble, she drove home and was reunited with her family. A spiritual happiness had touched her life.

Many others, young and old alike, share experiences of visiting the Nubble and sensing a happy, vital, energetic power or driving force that helps them overcome a feeling of depression or distress. This moving experience can be heartwarming, sentimental and stirring. It seems to linger in the area, a positive energy force as solid as the light tower itself. Life seems clear and less complicated from this vantage point overlooking the lighthouse.

The Nubble is one of the most visited and photographed lighthouses in America. Over the last few years several national companies have used Nubble Lighthouse as a background setting for television and print advertisements. The image of the Nubble has helped sell beer and automobiles. Maxwell House coffee featured it in one of their television commercials. Almost every major lighthouse calendar sold in the United States features Nubble Light. National Geographic, The Christian Science Monitor, and other national journals have published stories about the Nubble. When the light was automated in 1987, Peter Jennings broadcast a story about the lighthouse on his national ABC news program. The following day the Nubble was written up on the front page of the Wall Street Journal. Billboards depicting the lighthouse can be found in many states advertising a product or a place. Local newspapers and authors have written countless stories about this worthy landmark. The Nubble's tower has been used as a logo for educational institutions, banks, insurance companies and other large businesses. The Nubble is unique and the people of York, Maine are proud of its heritage.

In 1998 a historic event will take place when the town of York will officially receive the deed and title to the Cape Neddick Light Station. The Coast Guard is in the process of preparing the proper paperwork under a law authorized by the United States Congress that permits the transfer of Coast Guard light stations to private and civic groups. This will be a day of celebration.

The following section was written by Brenda Ahlgren and published in 1995 in the book "Nubble Light" by William O. Thomson. Brenda and her husband Russell Ahlgren occupied the Nubble Light House (Cape Neddick Light Station) from 1986 to 1987. Though her service took place in the last half of the twentieth century, many of her lighthouse experiences were similar to those of Connie Small who lived in lighthouses during the first half of the twentieth century.

48

Brenda Ahlgren's Memories:

It was very exciting for us to be assigned to Cape Neddick Light. It was like a dream come true - literally. A couple of months before the Coast Guard assigned us to the lighthouse we were living in Saco, Maine and we decided to go sightseeing. We drove south enjoying the quaint towns with the shops lining the streets and the awesome seacoast scenery. We came upon a little town called York, and found our way out to the Nubble Light. As we turned into the parking lot we were amazed at the sight of this beautiful lighthouse. At first glance you think the light is attached to the mainland, but as you approach closer you find this is not true. The way the light is situated it seems as if you can reach out and touch it, but alas you can only stand in awe of this historic landmark.

We were regular tourists that day taking pictures and all. As we drove home that day and for many days after, we shared our dreams of someday having a chance to live at an island lighthouse. You can imagine our surprise that a few months later, not only was Russ offered a transfer to a lighthouse, but to the very one we were dreaming of. We made our move in January 1986.

The lighthouse was equipped with many things we would need, so we had to make decisions of what we wanted or needed. The rest would have to go into storage. Everything was moved out by basket or boat. It was a very cold January day. We dressed in our new orange Coast Guard survival suits. A special survival suit was made for Christopher, our five month old son. It looked more like a sleeping bag - all you could see was his face. The suits protected us from the wind and the cold, but most important if the boat ever capsized it would protect us from the frigid Maine waters.

Our new mode of transportation was a three man rubber life raft. On calm days there was no problem getting back and forth, but any surf over two feet would begin to give us trouble.

49

Launching or beaching the boat could be dangerous. The timing between waves was important. I recall one time when Russ was taking a workman off the island it was getting rough. As I watched from the boathouse, they approached the mainland and Russ jumped out of the boat and held it for the worker to get out, but as a wave hit, Russ lost his footing and slid under the boat. All I could see were his hands holding on to the rope alongside the boat. In-between the waves he was able to get his footing and stood up. The workman got out of the boat unscathed. As Russ hopped back into the boat and rowed back to the island, I was able to take a breath again and help him haul the boat up to the boathouse. He was a sight, all soaking wet, and we laughed at the thought of the workman not coming back too soon!

For this reason Chris and I could go for up to a month without getting off the island because we decided that if it was too rough we wouldn't put Chris in the boat. We had some

Keeper Russ Ahlgren, Brenda and Christopher landing on the mainland in the rubber life raft.

wonderful friends on the mainland who would make a mail or grocery run for us when we were stranded for long periods of time.

Another way off the island was on moon tides. This is when tides run lower than normal. We had a chart that let us know what the tides were doing. As long as the water wasn't too rough you could walk off in knee deep or lower tides and not get knocked over. Some low tides would actually leave the split dry between the mainland and the island. We always tried to schedule visitors and workman to come over during these tides, otherwise we could not guarantee they could get on the island. This was also how we scheduled doctor's appointments and such. The only other link to the mainland was the basket. Sometimes we couldn't use the basket because rough seas would make it dangerous for anyone to stand on the mainland side. The pulley system would freeze up during ice storms and we would have to wait for it to thaw.

Our first week on the island was spent with the old keepers teaching us the many jobs that were expected of us. Every day the weather needed to be sent to Portsmouth Harbor Station. Every three hours between 6am to 6pm the present weather was called in, visibility, wind speed and direction, wave height, barometer, and outside temperature readings.

The flag must go up at 8am and down at sunset. Overall maintenance of the buildings and the light was Russ' responsibility. There also was office work for the lighthouse. Work logs were kept of the daily happenings. Work orders needed to be sent for repairs that were too big for us to handle and requests for supplies that were needed to fix anything we could handle. The lighthouse was also given a budget and Russ was responsible for this budget and how the money would be spent. The many storms added to the constant repairs on the island; as waves constantly pounded the boat ramp it was always in need of repair.

Russ couldn't do everything on his own. If he was out working, I would record and call the weather in. If Russ needed a hand I would be right there helping. We not only learned how to do things on our own, but we learned how to make do and do without. Running to the store or asking a neighbor for help was out of the question. Living on the island strengthened our trust and faith in each other. It taught us that with sheer determination many tasks can be accomplished.

Anytime Russ was away from the island it was my job to see that everything ran smoothly. One day Russ had to go up to his headquarters in Portland, Maine and had to stay overnight. It was my job to make sure the island was secure and the light was turned on and running properly. It was exciting and a little scary being on the island alone with Chris. In the earlier years some keepers' wives were paid a small amount for their work, but that was done away with and now man and wife are a total team living a special way of life.

When the command came out to make an inspection they would not only inspect Russ and his work, but our living quarters as well. If the house was not clean and orderly it could affect the outcome of his marks on the inspection report.

Getting off the island was always an event. If we went off as a family, we were allowed four hours at a time. We had to call Portsmouth Harbor Station and let them know when we left and when we returned. Most of our errands were done in town, but once every month or so I would go grocery shopping at Pease AFB in Portsmouth, New Hampshire. I would get enough groceries to last a month or so. We had a big freezer and storage cabinets in the laundry room. We froze extra gallons of milk and froze or canned fruit and vegetables. In the summer we had a garden that provided many vegetables for preserving purposes.

Upon my return from grocery shopping, I would call Russ from the parking lot to let him know I was back. Russ would put Chris in the backpack or in the cart and make his way down to the basket and send it over. I would park as close to the basket as possible, which was difficult in the summer with the parking lot full of tourists. Groceries had to be carried down the rocks and put into the basket (about six to eight bags fit at a time). Then by hand we would pulley the basket across to Russ who would unload the groceries into a pun cart we had. It usually took about four to five basket loads. Tourists were always curious. Some watched and some helped. I would answer questions as I walked back and forth, but never strayed from my work as we were always worried about weather and tide levels. We felt bad sometimes when we couldn't take the time to answer all their questions. We always enjoyed talking to people. We learned a lot about them as they did about us. It was interesting to hear people talk as I filled the basket. I heard one woman say, "Look, see what they eat!" - as if we ate different food because we live on a lighthouse. Another time I had a busload of tourists watching and I heard one say to another, "I wonder what it's like to do groceries in the winter?" and I answered, "Cold, very cold!" One day a young woman helped me carry groceries and when we were done she said she would never complain again about the two flights of stairs she had to climb to her apartment.

Another problem we had to deal with was wildlife. As we pulled the basket across the sea gulls would go along for a ride and try to peck at the bread and potatoes. Once the groceries were all across, Russ would pack up Chris and row over to get me. I would park the car in a space reserved for us and still answering

Andrew R. Thomson

Front Side of Nubble Light

Note the basket in front of the small white building on the top edge of the island. Also, note the distance from the boathouse up the stairs to the walkway and over to the residence.

the tourist's questions, I next had to change into my waders or survival suit (depending on the time of year). As I said, we enjoyed talking to people but we always had to stick to our objective or we would never get anything done. We were amazed at the number of people in the parking lot. It never seemed empty, even in the middle of the night there was at least one car there.

Once back on the island the boat needed to be put away and we walked the forty-two steps to the house. Grocery shopping wasn't done yet. We had to go down to the basket and retrieve the cart and it took both of us to pull it up to the house. Once the groceries were brought into the house and put away, dinner had to be made (we couldn't go out to eat). Needless to say it was usually early to bed.

People on the mainland would always get excited when we came out. We received a letter from a couple in Stow, Massachusetts and they wrote that on Mother's Day they were in the parking lot. They saw a delivery being made to the basket. They saw us come down to retrieve the basket and how Russ presented me with an azalea bush and how I returned with a thank you of a hug and a kiss for the lovely gift. Another couple had stayed at the cottages across the way spying on Russ every morning as he put up the flag, threw a stick for the dog, and went over to check the garden. Russ said he never realized his morning routine until it was pointed out to him. It felt funny to know how closely everyone was watching; it was like living in a "goldfish bowl." In time it was normal to walk around the yard and wave to people.

When the weather was good it was time for outside work and repairs. Once work was done it was time to play. We enjoyed being outside and took advantage of the beautiful location. We went for many walks on the island as a family and alone. We enjoyed our time together, but we also needed time to ourselves. Russ would go fishing in the Avon (rubber raft). I remember one time he went out, and he always took a radio in case of a problem, over the radio I heard him yell, "Whale!" I called back and asked him what he was talking about. He said a pilot whale had surfaced next to the Avon and then dove under the boat and resurfaced on the other side.

My free time was spent doing many types of crafts like needlepoint. I also enjoyed reading and writing in my journal. I also enjoyed rowing myself off the island. It wasn't very often as it took a lot of strength to maneuver the boat in rough seas. One calm winter day I had my survival suit on, with the hood, and I rowed across. I could hear the people in the parking lot say, "Here comes the lighthouse keeper." When I reached the rocks and had tied the boat I took off the hood and heard them say, "It's not the lighthouse keeper, it's his wife!"

We enjoyed our many walks around the island. We looked for anything that might have washed up. We would put Chris in the backpack and off we would go. (We did everything with Chris, no babysitters around.) One day we were looking under the seaweed to show Chris a starfish and we turned to show it to him and he already had one in his hand. He must have pulled it off one of the rocks when Russ bent over. On warm summer days we would go swimming and snorkeling off the boat ramp.

Rain was a welcomed sight as well as nice days. We collected rain water in the cisterns in the cellar. We had 4000

Andrew R. Thomson

South Side View of the Nubble

Despite the close proximity to land, the Nubble is a small island and can be a remote and isolated location during extended periods of bad weather.

gallon tanks. It sounded like a lot of water, but it goes fast if you are not careful. On a good rain storm we would run out and turn the catch buckets at the bottom of the rain gutters. These would funnel the water into the cisterns in the cellar. We would monitor the tanks and when they were near full we would get any extra laundry out of the way. We could enjoy a nice long shower and Chris would enjoy a full tub of water for his bath. When friends came to visit they would get a kick out of seeing how fast they could shower. We always watched our water consumption, because if we were low we would have to arrange to have water pumped to us by the York Beach Fire Department or a Coast Guard Cutter. It was a lot of work to run all the fire hoses to get this service.

As I said, our lives revolved around the weather. Fog meant isolation. It would have a kind of calming effect on you. Everything around you was quiet except the lone sound of the foghorn. Some days we wouldn't be able to see the parking lot, and on real foggy days we couldn't even see the flagpole in the front yard. Russ and I would joke that no one would know if we floated away until the fog lifted. It was always strange to find myself looking out the window even though I knew I couldn't see anything with all the fog.

One evening as I was preparing dinner, lo and behold there was a knock at the door. Now we haven't had anyone knock on the door or ring a doorbell in over a year, and wait - don't we live on an island? Needless to say it scared the heck out of us. It turned out to be two scuba divers who were lost in the fog. They started out diving at the mainland side and because of the fog never saw the island. They had come up on the southeastern side of the island and made their way up to the house. Russ helped them with their gear and took them back to the mainland in the rubber raft.

Another scuba diving incident happened on a beautiful day in March. We were out working in the back yard and could hear voices. We looked off the back of the island and saw two divers down on the rocks. We have heard that on the north side of the island there is a navigational pull that makes compasses go haywire. We climbed down the rocks to the divers and found them very exhausted and confused. One had bumped his head while trying to climb out onto the rocks. The swells were a good size and we were surprised they weren't seriously hurt. We carried their gear back over the rocks and Russ took them back to the mainland.

Andrew R. Thomson

The Back Side of the Nubble

Fog always seemed to confuse people. On another day we were out working in the yard and the fog rolled in rather quickly. All of a sudden we heard voices off the back of the island. We could make out a silhouette of a sixty foot sailboat and knew they were too close to the rocks below. We ran up and started yelling for them to turn away. We were happy when they heard our shouts and responded.

The major storms in New England are called Nor'easters. It was amazing to watch the strength of these storms as they came our way. In January 1987 we had a bad one. It was snowing very hard, the wind was blowing between sixty to seventy miles per hour, and the seas were ten to twelve feet high. I could never seem to comprehend how the sea could be so calm one moment and so angry the next. The wind was so strong it would keep you upright even though you were trying to lean into it. The tides were so high the water was up in the boathouse. As we looked out the office window to the north of the island, we could see that the tide was running higher than normal and had separated the north point of the island into smaller islands of its own. At night we could hear the waves pounding against the back of the island. It sounded like a severe thunderstorm. As we lay awake in bed we could only hear pounding waves and howling surf. The beam of the light flashed against the bedroom walls. The foghorn was on, but with all the noise it was hard to hear. I never seemed scared during these storms; I just enjoyed nature at its best.

When we woke the next morning we found the wind had not lessened any, but shifted drastically and had knocked the waves down to a mere three feet. At low tide we went for a walk on the island and found the waves had thrown two lobster traps into the middle of the rocks on the north point.

Another storm just like this past one returned at the end of the month. We received a lot of damage. We had to replace the walkway and cellar doors. We lost the garbage bin door with the wind. A section of the fence fell over and the boat ramp came

Andrew R. Thomson

View of the Keeper's House
The walkway up to the house is visible here and the height of the catwalk around the lantern room at the top of the tower.

loose. New storms always brought new adventures and new repairs.

It was Russ' job to keep the glass prisms on the Fresnel lens and the outside windows around the catwalk that protect the light clean at all times. This allowed for maximum visibility of the light to all boaters. The brass casing around the light also had to be polished and kept shining at all times.

We went through a tremendous ice storm one winter. The ice kept collecting on the windows of the light and had to be scraped every half hour. If the ice built up, the light could not be seen. We went up together as it was very windy and slippery on the catwalk. In the morning the island was sparkling in the sunshine. Russ went to put up the flag and had to slide down on his backside to the flagpole because it was too slippery to stand.

One of our memorable times was when the "Flying Santa Claus" came for a visit. We rushed outside early one December morning to the sound of a helicopter. We could see Santa sitting in the back as the pilot hovered over us. Next a big package was thrown down to us. It rolled down the hill and like little children we ran down after it. The wrapping paper had blown off and I told Russ to run and catch it because I saw something attached to it. The helicopter made one more pass and we waved good-bye as the pilot blew us a kiss. In all the excitement I could feel the tears well up in my eyes.

We ran inside to get warm. We were glad we had caught the wrapping paper as there was an envelope attached with a letter and drawings from Mrs. Curh's first grade class in Hull, Massachusetts. It was so exciting reading the letters and looking at the drawings. One that stands out it my mind was a drawing of the lighthouse with the family in the yard and Santa's sleigh dropping presents by parachute.

There were many questions from the students like "Does Chris have teeth?" "Do you see ships?" and "How do you get food?" As you can expect I enjoyed answering all their questions. The package was filled with toys for Chris, food for our holiday dinner, and even dog biscuits for Jade.

Another aspect of the light was the many requests for newspaper and television interviews. When the reports got out that we would be the last keepers of the lighthouse, because the lighthouse would be automated and closed, the calls for interviews started doubling. We realized we were becoming so called "celebrities." Just as Nathaniel Otterson and his family are known as the first keeper of the Nubble Light, we were becoming a part of history as the last lighthouse keepers.

A few months before the move, I made a very special trip off the island. Upon my return, as I was loading the basket, I yelled across to Russ, "Congratulations, you're going to be a Daddy again!" The grin he had on his face from ear to ear said it all. It was clear we would have a very special reminder of our tour on the lighthouse and her name would be Emily Marie.

As the day approached for the closing of the light and our move to our next assignment, we were saddened at the thought of leaving our island home. In the military you learn very fast not to get attached to any one place. The friends you make along the way are to be cherished and treasured for the moment. From day one we fell in love with the lighthouse, all our new friends, and our new way of life. The people of York and all the many tourists opened their arms and became our friends. Many of them still keep in touch with our family and the memories of the Nubble have moved with us many times over.

Family is very important to us and we found that being on the island enabled us to earn a living and enjoy our family at the same time. Russ and I learned to have trust and faith in each other. We built on our strengths and weaknesses and came to learn that together we could do anything.

It was ironic that the last week before the light was to be automated the island was surrounded by fog. The light and horn ran continuously. On our last night on the island we went for one last walk. We sat back on the rocks with Christopher between us and just watched the glow from that beautiful tall white tower and listened to the familiar drone of the horn we have come to enjoy. We felt that in its own special way the light was saying good-bye to family life on the island. As we sat there thinking back over our special adventure there was no way to hold back the tears. The lighthouse would now truly be one of isolation!

Brenda Ahlgren
Brenda and her husband Russell and their son Christopher were the last keepers to occupy the lighthouse before its automation in July of 1987.

PORTLAND HEAD LIGHT

Portland Head Light, Maine's oldest lighthouse, is located on the mainland in the town of Cape Elizabeth. The lighthouse was constructed on a headland, or large high section of rocks, known as Portland Head. Situated only three miles from Portland, Maine's largest city, it is one of the most visited lighthouses in America. The magnificent views of the rocky coast, open ocean, islands and breaking surf, and the exhilarating smell of pure salt sea air draw a million visitors a year from around the world to this picturesque public park.

Construction on the light began in earnest in 1790 when the first United States Congress appropriated $1500. The tower was built from rubble stone - rocks and boulders that were found in the area and hauled over to the site in wagons. Portland Head Light was the first lighthouse completed by the new government. It was first lit on January 10, 1791. President George Washington appointed the first keeper of the lighthouse, Captain Joseph Greenleaf.

United States Coast Guard Photo

Henry Wadsworth Longfellow was a frequent visitor to the lighthouse and befriended many of its keepers. In 1850 he published the poem entitled *The Lighthouse* which many people think was inspired by his visits to Portland Head Light.

The Lighthouse

The rocky ledge runs far into the sea,
and on its outer point, some miles away,
the lighthouse lifts its massive masonry,
A pillar of fire by night, of cloud by day.

Even at this distance I can see the tides,
Upheaving, break unheard along its base,
A speechless wrath, that rises and subsides
in the white tip and tremor of the face.

And as the evening darkens, lo! how bright,
through the deep purple of the twilight air,
Beams forth the sudden radiance of its light,
with strange, unearthly splendor in the glare!

Not one alone: from each projecting cape
And perilous reef along the ocean's verge,
Starts into life a dim, gigantic shape,
Holding its lantern o'er the restless surge.

Like the great giant Christopher it stands
Upon the brink of the tempestuous wave,
Wading far out among the rocks and sands,
The night o'er taken mariner to save.

And the great ships sail outward and return
Bending and bowing o'er the billowy swells,
And ever joyful, as they see it burn
They wave their silent welcomes and farewells.

They come forth from the darkness, and their sails
Gleam for a moment only in the blaze,
And eager faces, as the light unveils
Gaze at the tower, and vanish while they gaze.

The mariner remembers when a child,
on his first voyage, he saw it fade and sink;
And when returning from adventures wild,
He saw it rise again o'er ocean's brink.

Steadfast, serene, immovable, the same
Year after year, through all the silent night
Burns on forevermore that quenchless flame,
Shines on that inextinguishable light!

It sees the ocean to its bosom clasp
The rocks and sea-sand with the kiss of peace:
It sees the wild winds lift it in their grasp,
And hold it up, and shake it like a fleece.

The startled waves leap over it; the storm
Smites it with all the scourges of the rain,
And steadily against its solid form
press the great shoulders of the hurricane.

The sea-bird wheeling round it, with the din
of wings and winds and solitary cries,
Blinded and maddened by the light within,
Dashes himself against the glare, and dies.

A new Prometheus, chained upon the rock,
Still grasping in his hand the fire of Jove,
it does not hear the cry, nor heed the shock,
but hails the mariner with words of love.

"Sail on!" it says: "sail on, ye stately ships!
And with your floating bridge the ocean span;
Be mine to guard this light from all eclipse.
Be yours to bring man neared unto man.

The waters off Portland Head Light have been the gravesite of many large ships. Keeper Elder M. Jordan was the keeper when the *Bohemian* went aground on February 22, 1864. After a slow voyage due to rough seas and stormy weather, the *Bohemian*, on its way from Liverpool, England to Portland made for Portland Head Light. Two hundred and eighteen people were on board. Captain Borland, apparently confused by hazy conditions, did not know his exact position and his ship struck Alden Rock. Engine power was lost as the ship's boilers were flooded by the sea gushing through the hull. The ship traveled about two more miles, coming to a halt at Broad Cove. As the passengers tried to escape the damaged ship, one of the lifeboats was swamped. Forty-two men and one woman drowned in the frigid water. One mother tied her little baby onto her back and swam safely to shore. Many of the passengers were Irish immigrants hoping to find a better life in America but it was certainly a rough start. Twelve days later a northeast gale sent the rest of the ship to the bottom. Its cargo of china, silk, tea, silverware and large bolts of woolens, cotton goods and satins washed ashore.

In the storm of 1869 twenty vessels went down to their watery grave. The strong gale and giant waves ripped the Portland Head Light's three-quarter-ton fog bell from its secure fasteners and propelled it into a ravine several feet away. The heavy seas smashed many windows in the main structure itself. Powerful whirling winds and a violent sea show no mercy. During storms like this the keepers and their families went into the tower for security. They brought food, water, coffee, pillows, blankets and all of their pets with them, hoping the storm would pass quickly and that their home would still be standing when they emerged. The tumultuous sea often destroyed buildings around the lighthouse, and the stone tower offered the best chance for survival.

Keeper Joshua Freeman Strout rescued the victims of a major shipwreck at Portland Head on December 24, 1886. The *Annie C. Maguire*, a three masted bark registered in Buenos Aires, struck the ledge next to the lighthouse tower. Breached by the jagged rocks, the ship lay helpless as the surf broke around its hull. The ship had turned into the harbor as a storm began building at sea. Because the weather was not extreme (the crew reported seeing the lighthouse clearly) and there were no problems with the ship, the cause of the wreck has remained a mystery. Bound for Quebec, it was sailing "in ballast" – probably carrying bags of heavy sand to stabilize her and give the captain more control. The ship was also under attachment because its Canadian owners owed money to creditors. The local sheriff had been contacted to serve papers if the ship arrived in Portland, and he notified Keeper Strout to be on the watch for the vessel.

The captain of the *Annie C. Maguire* was a man by the name of O'Neil. On board were his wife, two mates and a nine man crew. Captain O'Neil claimed he was heading for the main channel, but anyone looking out to sea said it appeared that he was aiming for the ledge. The keeper tried desperately to alert the captain but failed. His son Joseph, an experienced seaman himself, grabbed a life line and when the ship struck he threw the rope out to the crew. When the line was secured, the Strouts and some volunteers rigged up an ordinary ladder which was used as a gangplank between the shore and the ledge. One by one, Mrs. O'Neil, the crew and Captain climbed on the ledge and crossed the ladder to safety. It had to have been a frightening and strenuous climb - crawling between the rungs, thirty feet above the raging sea that pounded the rocks below, knowing that just one slip would cause instant death. The exhausting, formidable task was accomplished without injury under the unyielding and fastidious direction of the Strout family.

After the crewmembers of the *Annie C. Maguire* were brought inside the warm keeper's quarters, the sheriff served the papers to Captain O'Neil. The captain was concerned that he had lost a sizeable sum of money in a sea chest that had been left onboard the wreck. He was relieved to find out that Mrs. O'Neil, a frugal and well organized woman, had taken the money and put it in the handbag she carried to shore. The crew had also removed two cases of scotch whiskey.

As word of the wreck spread through town, many Cape Elizabeth and Portland residents visited the site to watch the ship slowly break apart. Some gathered bits and pieces of the boat as the debris washed in with the waves. After a few days, the captain settled the business with the local authorities and he was free to return to Canada. The Strouts had done their job and they did it well. Their only complaint was that the unexpected guests had eaten most of the station's food supply.

Captain Joshua Strout served as keeper of Portland Head from 1869 until 1904 when he was replaced by his son Joseph, who served at the station until 1928. Today a marker is painted on the sharp spiked edges of the cliff next to the lighthouse where the ship went down. It reads, "Annie C. Maguire shipwrecked here Christmas Eve 1886."

LIGHTHOUSE HAUNTINGS

What is a ghost? What is considered a haunting? Asking different people these questions will generate many different answers. As kids, we all remember a big vacant mansion with broken windows, creaking doors, and shutters that blew in the wind. Some of these old haunts were near abandoned graveyards, adding to the mystery. More than one brave youngster accepted a challenge to climb the stairs, enter the structure and explore the darkness inside. Soon the sounds of the rushing wind, creaking blinds, the bangs, groans and slams were amplified, causing even the least active imagination to create a wild scenario of impending doom. As fear mounted, it became a test of strength and endurance to stay inside. Most of the children ran back outside long before they encountered an apparition. This is how a lot of people still think of ghosts, but many sane and sound people who have had a ghostly experience know differently.

No one can predict exactly when a ghost will appear or in what form it will make itself known. It can be visible – a cloud of mist or a human figure drifting through a room. It can be a fragrance in the air or just a presence sensed or felt. It can also be a voice or sound. People who have experienced a ghost, and those who have lived with one, agree that it is probably an energy force left behind when someone died, usually by violent means - a suicide, murder, or traumatic accident. Certain sensitive individuals may be able to receive or "tune in" this energy force, just as a radio or television can be tuned to a specific frequency. Many keepers of lighthouses have reported these ghostly apparitions moving in and out of the towers or keeper's homes, and they have felt their presence in the outbuildings and on the grounds around their stations.

67

A FEW OF NEW ENGLAND'S LEGENDARY HAUNTED LIGHTHOUSES

Light Station	Built	Location
Seguin Light	1795	Georgetown, ME
Ram Island Light	1883	Boothbay Harbor, ME
Isles of Shoals	1821	Portsmouth, NH
Minots Ledge Light	1850	Cohasset, MA
Owls Head Light	1825	Owls Head, ME
Block Island S.E.	1875	Block Island, RI
Wood Island Light	1808	Biddeford, ME
Hendricks Head	1829	Southport, ME
New London Ledge	1909	Avery Point, CT
Boon Island Light	1800	York, ME

Many unexplained experiences have occurred at the ten New England lighthouses listed above. Sightings of ghosts or apparitions have terrified some witnesses. Mysterious sounds and activities have left others chilled to the bone. At times a strange feeling of a spirit's presence lingered with the witnesses as they completed their regular duties and chores. These episodes might be whispers from the past, messages from former occupants who are not yet ready to leave the lighthouse. Perhaps they still have tasks they need to complete. Maybe they are afraid they would be leaving someone else behind. But are these experiences real? Do apparitions really roam about in these locations for their own unexplainable reasons? These questions are often asked, but seldom answered with provable facts.

Most of these lighthouses were built in the nineteenth century when sailors guided wind powered ships through the deep open seas – the superhighways of the past. When the sea lanes ended and the destination port loomed on the horizon, the unmarked waters of the harbor had to be approached with caution. Hidden ledges, jagged rocks, small islands or sand bars were potential disasters as the ships passed. These hazards were soon marked by lighthouses; beautiful but solitary guardians; beacons of hope. Sailors watched for the beacons with spyglasses and strained their ears to hear the fog bells and horns. These were the sights and sounds of faith penetrating fog, snow, and darkness, which guided them safely into the harbor.

The mariners relied upon these signals and trusted that they would function at all times. The keepers and their families devoted themselves to the task, maintaining a never ending vigil over the tower beacon and the bell. Despite the physical hardships from fierce storms or intense cold, despite the mental anguish from desperate loneliness and isolation, the oil fired lamps burned brightly and the bells tolled through the fog. The keepers had personalities of steel. Some died performing their duty in acts of bravery; some were victims of tragic accidents; others died quietly while maintaining their watch. It is entirely possible that some of these dedicated souls refused to leave their posts and that their apparitions continue to haunt the lighthouses today.

THE GHOST AT SEGUIN LIGHT STATION

Seguin Island Light Station is one of the oldest light stations in Maine. Established in 1795 it is also one of the highest stations, rising one hundred and eighty-six feet above sea level. The area is very busy with sea traffic entering the Kennebec and Sheepscott Rivers and it is one of the foggiest locations along the coast - its foghorn is activated an average of one hundred and twenty days a year. The island is about a half mile long and from the air it resembles a large turtle, its feet and head outlined by rounded coves.

The Seguin lighthouse is one of the stations where keepers have reported seeing and hearing strange events. Legend has it that in the mid 1800's a keeper was assigned to the island with his young wife and while the keeper did his chores, his wife would play the piano. At first, the keeper enjoyed listening to the music as the soft delicate sounds of her playing drifted into the tower. As time went on however, and loneliness set in, it seems the woman started playing her favorite song over and over again. Soon she was playing the same tune continuously for hours without stopping.

The keeper tried to get her to stop without success. He pleaded with her to at least play a different song, but by the time he would climb back up the spiral stairs into the tower, the same familiar irritating chords would invade the watch room and assault his ears. She played with more intensity and the noise grew louder and less melodic. Finally he snapped. He ran down the stairs and without thinking, grabbed an axe and ran into the house swinging it wildly. He attacked the piano, smashing it into pieces and then turned the axe on his wife. It was a grisly violent murder. No one knows whether the keeper experienced a sense of remorse, or if his burst of insanity continued, but he then took his own life. It has been reported by ships passing the island on calm quiet nights that a strange tune could be heard in the distance – over and over again.

In the early 1970's and again in the 1980's a team of Coast Guard personnel was assigned to the island. During conversations the author had with some of these men, they revealed some

Seguin Island Duplex Keeper's House

interesting stories. One boatswain's mate related several encounters with a ghost he referred to as "the old captain." The visible figure seems to feel right at home in the station. He has been seen often, climbing the winding iron stairway up to the tower and once he was standing behind one of the men during a game of checkers. A young girl was also seen running up and down the stairs. She waved to the men on several occasions and some heard her laughter. She and the old captain were both spotted in the area of the island between the lighthouse and the powerful foghorn. Sounds ranging from groans to laughter have been heard in this area, which seems to be particularly haunted. It has been reported that this young girl died on the island and her parents buried her near the generator house.

Another person reported hearing the sound of a bouncing ball, similar to a basketball, coming from the upstairs bedroom. When the crew went to investigate, nothing was found. Some of the men also reported that cold spots brushed by them as they were polishing brass or doing other maintenance work. Pea jackets were taken off hooks and thrown on the floor. Tools were missing and then they would reappear where they belonged.

The steep incline from the boat landing to the building complex makes Seguin one of the most difficult lighthouses to visit. Supplies were pulled up to the house on a long trolley track by an engine called a donkey motor. In 1985, as the light station was being prepared for automation, a work crew was busy packing all of the items in the house for shipment to the mainland. At the end of the long day, when everything was crated and boxed, the crew retired for the evening.

In the middle of the night, the warrant officer was abruptly awakened when his bed suddenly started shaking violently. As he snapped into consciousness he saw an apparition at the bottom of the bed; an old man dressed in oil skins was rattling the footboard. "Don't take the furniture," the old captain murmured. "Please leave my house alone."

The warrant officer bolted out of bed and ran into the next room. Assuming he had just had an intense nightmare, he forced himself to forget the vision and get some sleep. The next morning the men started loading all of the boxes and crates onto a skid which would be gently lowered along the trolley tracks to the landing. The warrant officer never mentioned his dream to the others. When the last box was placed on the trolley and the load was secured, he gave the order to start the donkey engine. The men watched the process as the cargo inched its way down the track toward the ocean below.

About a third of the way down, the motor stopped cold. A moment later the chain holding the skid broke apart and the load rapidly accelerated down the rails. It flew off the bottom of the

track and hit the rough ocean, immediately sinking upon the impact and everything was lost.

To this day, the warrant officer believes that the old captain was somehow involved in the mechanical

The Seguin Trolley

failure. It is a common belief that ghosts do not like change and one can't help but wonder if the apparition wanted to keep his belongings on the island. Perhaps the old man enlisted the aid of the young girl to stop the men from removing their possessions.

RAM ISLAND LIGHT

Ram Island Light, built in 1883, sits on a remote island just off Boothbay Harbor, Maine. Several years before the light was constructed, an old salt was driven up on the rocks during bad weather. The poor soul had no way of alerting anyone to his dire predicament and he soon died of exposure. Over the years following the tragedy, local fishermen reported strange occurrences in the area. Fires were spotted on the beach at night but no charred debris or ashes were found in the morning. During foul weather, sailors who were dangerously approaching the island were warned off by signal whistles when there were no such whistles on Ram Island. Other locals have reported seeing a strange figure or apparition aimlessly roaming the island. The old salt might have stayed behind to help his fellow mariners avoid a fate similar to his own.

United States Coast Guard Photo

Ram Island Light

This was one of the last lighthouses built on the coast of Maine. Before construction in 1883, shipwrecks were so frequent that local fishermen took it upon themselves to light a lantern and hang it on a pole from a dory anchored off the island.

ISLES OF SHOALS

Andrew R. Thomson

Star Island - Isles of Shoals

Located about six miles from the entrance to Portsmouth Harbor, the Isles of Shoals is a group of small islands that straddle the border of Maine and New Hampshire. The chain stretches for about three miles from Duck Island in the north to White Island in the south and includes Smuttynose, Appledore, Cedar, and Star islands. The shoals were always a hazard to mariners in bad weather and in 1821, the Isles of Shoals lighthouse was built on White Island to mark the area. First settled in the 1600's as a small but successful fishing community, the islands have a rich history that includes visits from pirates, raids by the local Native American tribes, shipwrecks on the rocky outcroppings, and murders in the small cottage-style homes. Legendary stories of ghosts and apparitions that haunt the islands are abundant.

One of the apparitions reported most often on the islands is a mysterious lady dressed in white. She is often seen roaming near the rocky shore and some folks have reported hearing her crying softly toward the sea, "He shall return. He shall return." Legend has it that she is one of the wives of the notorious pirate Blackbeard. Supposedly, he stopped at the island to bury some of his treasure and was almost captured. During his hasty departure, he left the young lady in white behind.

United States Coast Guard Photo

White Island - Isles of Shoals

In 1724, an Indian raiding party paddled out to the islands from the mainland. Betty Moody quickly grabbed her two infant children and ran to a cave near the shoreline. She crawled toward the back and hid in the darkness, waiting for the raiders to leave. If discovered, she and her children could be kidnapped or murdered. She tried desperately to keep her frightened children silent. At this point, some people say that she suffocated the children by holding them so tightly to muffle their cries. Others have said that she stabbed the infants to avoid capture, and thus spared them from a fate worse than death. To this day, visitors to the island have reported seeing an apparition of Betty and her children in the area known as "Betty Moody's Cave."

In the mid 1800's Nancy Underhill was a young schoolteacher on the islands. She used to have a favorite rock at the end of the island where she would often sit reading, writing or correcting her students' papers. On one occasion as she sat engrossed in a book, a huge wave rose up from the sea and swept her off the rocks. Her lifeless body washed up on the mainland a couple of days later. The vision of a young woman has been seen frequently on the rocky ledge known as "Miss Underhill's Chair."

Former keepers at the Isles of Shoals Light reported a strange event that happened on more than one occasion. During what appeared to be a beautiful calm day, they heard a soft strange voice which apparently came from the foot of the ramp next to the keeper's house. It was a nervous, restless female voice which seemed to be calling out a warning. None of the keepers could make out the words she was speaking and the message lasted for several minutes. Each time the voice was heard, the weather changed dramatically within two hours, and a storm would pass over the islands. Perhaps it is the voice of the pirate's wife, warning him to be careful as he returns to the island to rescue her. It could be Miss Underhill telling the keeper's to watch out for the raging surf that will break over the island during the impending storm.

Claudia Crafts

MINOTS LEDGE LIGHT

Minots Ledge Light is considered the most dangerous lighthouse on the New England Coast. The original tower was constructed in 1850 to keep ships away from the Cohasset Reefs, a series of deadly submerged rocks that were a great navigational hazard to ships sailing off the coast of Cape Cod. The tower was completely surrounded by water and the remote location made construction difficult.

On April 16, 1851 a severe Nor'easter raged along the Massachusetts coast. As the storm approached the ledge, the seas rose rapidly. The two keepers on duty stayed in the watch room and tended to the light as the surf pounded the tower, shaking its foundation. As the storm intensified, the tower became less stable. Fearing that they would be washed into the sea, the keepers grabbed a sledge hammer and pounded on the signal bell in a desperate attempt to alert someone to their plight. The base of the tower started to crumble under the force of the sea and the men kept hitting the bell, sending a farewell signal to their families on the shore. Finally the lighthouse collapsed and the two doomed keepers were swept away by the violent sea. Their bodies washed up on Gull Island and were retrieved the next day.

A ninety-seven foot tower was built over the same location and was first lit on August 22, 1860. Before it was automated in 1947, many keepers assigned to the second tower reported hearing strange sounds in the lighthouse. Perhaps it was the wind or the sea vibrating and shaking the structure. They described the sounds as a rhythmic pounding, like a message or code. It could be the spirits of the two brave men who died so tragically while performing their duty during the storm.

United States Coast Guard Photo

Minots Ledge Light

Construction of this tower (a replacement for one which was destroyed in 1851) started in 1855 and took five years to complete. It is one hundred and fourteen feet high and was built by interlocking over a thousand blocks of granite in such a way that the pounding surf would actually strengthen the structure. Ira Winn, of Portland, Maine, constructed the brass platform deck around the top of the tower.

OWLS HEAD LIGHT

Owls Head Light was built in 1825 on a headland near the entrance to Rockland Harbor. The tower, separated from the keeper's house by a long stairway, is only twenty feet tall but it sits on the promontory one hundred feet above the high water line. Surrounded by spruce trees, this location is rich in scenery.

Like all lighthouses, it was once manned by a "wickie" - an affectionate name given by Coast Guard personnel to the old keepers who once served under the Lighthouse Service. These old timers were given the rank of Chief Petty Officer when they were transferred into the Coast Guard and they had the distinction of wearing a cap with crossed oars on the emblem. They had all tended the wicks that kept the beacon lights shining. Some of the old wickies reported seeing the image of a keeper who had died on duty at Owls Head roaming through the lighthouse, attempting to perform his duties as though he were still on watch.

Recent keepers discovered that the old wickie is still on duty and that he likes to keep the heat down. The place was always frigid. They would set the temperature to a comfortable level and go about their tasks. A short time later, feeling chilled, they discovered that the thermostat had been reset much lower. Apparently the old keeper felt that conserving the lighthouse fuel supply was important.

The white keeper's house sits at the bottom of a two hundred foot boardwalk that slants up to the high point of land and the tower. Keepers have reported finding footprints in fresh snow on the walkway leading up to the light but not returning. Footprints have also appeared in the early morning dew and vanished near the tower. Someone was climbing the walkway but his identity remained a mystery. One keeper reported that when he followed the prints he found the large steel door on the tower open and swinging. The door had been locked the night before. As he entered the tower he felt as if someone was with him, breathing on the back of his neck. The keeper saw a figure out of the corner of his eye, but when he turned toward it, the figure disappeared.

Many strange things have been reported throughout the property. At times the case around the Fresnel lens had been opened and it appeared that someone had tried to light the lantern. Brass had been polished without explanation. Silverware rattled and glasses vibrated for no reason. Doors have slammed shut and some keepers have seen the shadow of an old man gliding by the windows. No one seems to know who the old captain is, but he seems content to stay at the lighthouse and remain on duty.

There is also a legend about an older, unidentified lady who has been seen in the kitchen of the keeper's house. The "Little Lady" as she is known, usually appears when the ship's clock strikes eleven or thirteen. She has gray hair and a beautiful face and seems loving and kind - a happy spirit who conveys a certain calmness. When her presence is felt or her apparition is seen, a feeling of joy and well-being comes over those who are present. They agree that she must have been a wonderful person and that they would have liked to have known her.

United States Coast Guard Photo

Owls Head Lighthouse

BLOCK ISLAND (SOUTHEAST) LIGHT

United States Coast Guard Photo

Block Island - Southeast

Two hundred and one feet above sea level, Block Island – Southeast stands on the top of Mohegan Bluffs about twelve miles off the coast of Rhode Island. The red brick keeper's house and sixty-seven foot tower were completed on February 1, 1875. The beacon light flashes a green signal, which is unusual for a New England Lighthouse.

Legends abound about a keeper's wife who haunts this lighthouse. In the early 1900's the keeper on duty grew excessively tired of his wife, perhaps from spending too much time with her at the station. In a fit of rage, he reportedly threw her off the round staircase just beneath the lantern room at the top of the tower. The woman's spirit now roams the house. She does not seem to bother other women on the property, but she takes great joy in annoying the men who have been stationed here. There have been many reports of her creating disturbances or causing a fuss. Everyone in the area knows of her presence and she is a good topic of conversation.

The kitchen area seems to be one of her favorite rooms in the residence. She has been known to throw objects at some of the keepers. Food has flown off the table and landed across the room; dishes have been smashed for no reason. One keeper reports that he was cooking some food on a medium low heat. He left the kitchen for a moment and when he returned, he found his food burning in the pan with the burner turned up to its full height. This apparition appears to have a temper.

She has been known to constantly rearrange furniture and artifacts around the rooms. Male keepers have returned to their bedroom and found the entire room turned around. Beds have been moved, chairs have been repositioned, and pictures on the bureau have been turned upside down. Some keepers have found their clothes removed from the closet and thrown across the bed. Bureau drawers have been opened during the night and socks were flung around the room. She lifts beds off the floor and shakes them violently. She has been known to chase men from room to room. Another light keeper was repeatedly harassed, until one night he was chased out of his bedroom and through the house. He ran outside to the grounds and the door slammed shut and locked behind him. Dressed only in his underwear, he was embarrassed when he had to call for help to get back inside his quarters.

Keepers have reported cold spots in various parts of the house or in specific corners of rooms. The entire room could be toasty warm, but one spot would always be chilled. The apparition has been seen or felt moving rapidly up and down the staircase, to the point where some keepers have pressed their bodies to the walls as she raced by, feeling perhaps that she might have a vengeful desire to throw them from the stairs.

Because the cliffs were losing their battle with the sea and deteriorating rapidly, in 1993 the Block Island (Southeast) Light Station complex was moved about two hundred and fifty feet back from its original location. Often when a haunted structure is moved, the spirit goes away. It will be interesting to see if the old keeper's wife stays in the brick house and tower and becomes a part of its new location. Time will tell.

WOOD ISLAND LIGHT

Wood Island Light was first lit in 1808. Standing seventy-one feet above the water on the eastern tip of Wood Island, it marks the entrance to the Saco River. The island is located approximately one half mile from the eastern shore of Biddeford Pool, Maine and about a mile from the entrance to the river. Although it is located close to land, the station has endured many storms as it is completely exposed to the full fury of the Atlantic Ocean. At one time the area around the island was a rich fishing ground full of mackerel, herring, and lobster. Many old salts spent a lot of time in these waters, and they have told some interesting tales. One story about a murder and suicide has convinced some of them that the island is haunted.

At the end of the 1800's a powerfully strong young lobster man from Biddeford Pool moved into a shack on Wood Island. Along with his occupation of fishing, he was also a special deputy sheriff. Another young man also took up residence on the island, a twenty-five year old drifter and heavy drinker. One afternoon when the deputy sheriff returned from the mainland to the island, he found the twenty-five year old drunk and unruly. The young man was waving a rifle around and pointing it at the deputy. The sheriff tried to disarm the man, but in the ensuing struggle the gun went off and killed the constable. The drunk stumbled up to the lighthouse and tried to surrender himself to the keeper, who told him to go to the mainland and report the shooting to the police. Instead, he returned to his crude shed on the west end of the island and shot himself in the head with the rifle. He died instantly.

Shortly after this time, a ghostly figure has been seen, and its presence has been felt, by people on the island. He appears to be friendly and most of his "tricks" are good natured, leading many to suspect that he is the ghost of the burly lobster man. The keepers at the lighthouse learned to live with these strange occurrences as though the perpetrator was a member of their crew. Window shades were lowered. Many strange unexplainable noises and banging sounds were heard. The most common trick was opening and closing doors. Doors that had been locked were later found open and swinging on their hinges, while doors that had been braced open were slammed shut. Sometimes a door would open by itself when someone approached it.

United States Coast Guard Photo

Wood Island Light

The island has had an interesting history. In the early 1900's during one winter gale, three schooners were sunk on the island and several of the crew drowned. Many other ships have been ruined on the rocks losing crewmembers. One night a ship was driven up on the rocks and when a rescue party arrived at the site they realized that the captain's wife was suffering from smallpox. The rescuers disappeared quickly, but the lighthouse keeper and his wife prepared a temporary shelter in one of the outbuildings and nursed the woman back to health. Smallpox was a dreaded disease and the captain and his wife were lucky to find such a benevolent keeper.

Wood Island has always been an island full of intrigue. The murders, severe storms and many shipwrecks provided some interesting stories for the keepers when they left the lighthouse. One old man tried to raise chickens on the island, but he soon found out that the chickens weren't good company and the solitude took its toll. For weeks he was seen pacing back and forth on the beach until he rowed to shore, rented a room in a boarding house, and then took his own life by jumping out of the third story window. Other residents of this island have endured hard times. Some of the squatters lost their ramshackle homes when an old drunkard carelessly discarded some matches and burned the structures to the ground. At one time the island had a distillery and a pub but this was burned down by some drunken fisherman. Wood Island Light has survived, but its colorful history lends itself to feelings that some of the spirits still linger from the past.

HENDRICKS HEAD

The beacon at Hendricks Head Light first flashed in 1829, marking the entrance to the Sheepscot River in Maine. From the lantern room forty-three feet above the ocean, the keepers of this light saw a schooner pounded to pieces just off the rocky shore in the 1870's. All of the crew and passengers on board the wreck perished except for a tiny young girl. Her mother had anticipated their impending doom and she lashed the baby between two mattresses with the hopes that she would float safely to shore. The keeper rescued the child and he and his wife later adopted her. As they had just buried their own young daughter a few weeks before, they considered the baby a gift from God. She grew up and lived a normal, happy life.

In the early 1900's a mysterious woman was walking along the beach. Some of the local folks spoke to her, but she remained silent. No one recognized her, but they said she seemed very refined. She was an attractive young woman in her early twenties. The next day her body was found washed up on the beach, some heavy objects were strapped around her waist. She was buried in the local cemetery. Had she committed suicide? Was she a victim of foul play? Had she been murdered by rum runners who were sneaking their illegal cargo on shore? The circumstances of her death remain a mystery. But over the last sixty years, a young woman has been seen pacing the beach north of the lighthouse where she drowned. People try to speak to her, but she doesn't answer. Her identity is unknown. Footprints are visible in the morning, as though some poor lost soul had been wandering aimlessly along the beach throughout the night.

United States Coast Guard Photo

Hendricks Head Light

NEW LONDON LEDGE

New London Ledge is fifty-eight feet above the water of the Thames River at the entrance to New London Harbor in Connecticut. The light was first activated on November 10, 1909. The station was built on a dangerous reef and the entire lighthouse and living area sits on a fifty foot square of concrete completely surrounded by water. The foundation of this small light station is embedded into the ledge. The structure is sturdy and seems to have been built with great care and attention to detail. But the most striking feature of the building is that it is small.

One early keeper of the light was named "Ernie." He was happily married when he moved into the tiny three story lighthouse with his wife. He thought he had a marriage made in heaven and the two of them would be together for twenty-four hours a day - every day. Working side by side they took good care of their little home and dutifully maintained the beacon.

United States Coast Guard Photo

New London Ledge Lighthouse

There was not much breathing room in the close quarters and apparently the beauty of the place was not enough to overcome the feelings of confinement. It was too much for Ernie's wife and it is said that she ran off with a local ship captain and left Ernie alone to tend the light. When he realized what had happened, Ernie climbed up to the top of the roof and ended his life by jumping into the frigid water below.

Ernie's apparition still roams the building. Keepers have reported such things as the house lights being turned on and off; the foghorn has been turned on at unusual times; items in the house have been cleaned or polished. This is all credited to Ernie. The keepers have heard strange noises in the hall, and when they investigated the sounds they felt a cold spot and an eerie stillness seemed to prevail. It is quite obvious that Ernie does not want to leave this unique light station, despite the fact that his spirit must be despondent because of the actions of his wife.

Ernie seems to be a part of the lighthouse family at New London Ledge. His spirit doesn't talk and he has never harmed anyone but his energy force is strong. He appears at the top of stairs for a few seconds and then vanishes. When his spirit is present, scraping sounds, bumps and soft footsteps can be heard. If his wife had only known how much he would miss her, would she still have run away?

BOON ISLAND LIGHT

In 1855 the present light tower was first lit on Boon Island, a small three acre rocky ledge located almost seven miles off the coast of York Beach, Maine. At one hundred and thirty-seven feet above sea level, it is the tallest lighthouse in the state. It was one of the most barren, remote and challenging light stations assigned to a keeper. The lack of accessibility to the island meant that all of the keepers at Boon have experienced long periods of complete isolation. Before radio and telephones, their only communication with the mainland was by carrier pigeon.

Storms passing over the island were tests of endurance. Heavy seas threw huge boulders, many weighing tons, across the island. Some came to rest against the doors of the house or the tower, trapping the people inside. The entire complex of out buildings including the residence, hen house, storage unit, boardwalk, and landing area, have been washed into the sea during fierce gales and storms. During these storms the keepers and their families sought refuge in the solid granite tower.

Andrew R. Thomson

Boon Island Light

One hundred and sixty-seven iron stairs spiral up from the base of the tower to the watch room. A metal ladder leads from there to the lantern room above. As the keepers completed their lonely watch at the top of the structure, it is a small wonder that the noise of the wind whistling around the glass and the amplified sounds that echoed through the damp dark tower did not stimulate their imaginations to create vivid stories of spirits and ghosts. Some keepers have reported strange crying sounds, but Boon Island does not seem to have many of these stories. One tale that has been told by the locals however, does stand out.

Sometime after the present tower was built, a young keeper was assigned to the station. He took his new wife with him to the island, and the two seemed to have an ongoing honeymoon as their relationship blossomed while they worked together at the light. Four months after they started their tour of duty, a severe midwinter gale came up. The keeper went outside to secure the island boat. The frigid surf had covered the boulders near the landing with a coating of ice. The young man slipped, plunged into the ocean and drowned. His wife had witnessed the accident and ran to the shore, but she was too late. She had no one to scream to for help. All she could do was grab onto his frozen arms and drag him back up to the house. She placed his body in the base of the tower and collapsed next to her dead spouse. She had never felt so totally alone. The terrible stormy seas tossed huge boulders up against the tower. The air was frigid and a thick sea fog had formed on the surface of the ocean.

Despite her horrible frightening situation, the poor helpless soul left her husband and climbed the one hundred and sixty-

Andrew R. Thomson

seven steps to the lantern room and tended the light. For the next five days she climbed the spiral staircase every few hours to make sure the wicks stayed lit and then she climbed back down to sit beside her husband's corpse. With no food or water, her strength finally gave out and she did not make the climb. The beacon ran out of fuel and the light was extinguished. Some local fishermen went out to the island to investigate. The young woman was near death, but she was still holding her dead husband's hand. She was returned to the mainland, but never recovered from the dreadful experience; the anguish of this frightening event had taken its toll. Perhaps her cries still echo in the cold damp tower - or maybe it is just the cry of a lonely sea gull passing in the night.

Andrew R. Thomson

CONCLUSION

As Samuel Adams Drake once wrote, "There is nothing that moves the imagination like a lighthouse." Lighthouses have always been bewitching. Their remote locations are at the end of solid land, on the edge of the tumultuous sea. Their beacons cast an eerie glow in the fog and mist, and an eternal light that offers hope, security and guidance. The tolling of their bells and the dirge of their foghorns can be soothing, mysterious, and disconcerting at the same time. Their history is rich with tales of human suffering and stories of unbelievable courage and dignity.

The lighthouse keeper's way of life is gone; their names and deeds are now recorded in history. Only legend and folklore have made lighthouse living romantic. Whether these brave guardians of the shore were facing perilous natural hazards or long periods of dreadful calm and intense isolation, they summoned up the strength to do what they had to do. We all owe these keepers a deep debt of gratitude.

Rendering From United States Coast Guard Photo

Author

Bill Thomson is a native New Englander, residing in Kennebunk, Maine. After teaching thirty-three years in the history department at Salem State College, Salem, Massachusetts, he retired Professor Emiritus in 1996. He has written many books about New England's heritage. As well as producing his own documentaries which have been shown on major New England television stations, he has also appeared on six national lighthouse programs shown on PBS, Discovery, Travel, HGTV and the History Channel. He lectures at many local schools and civic groups. His expertise is "Human Interest History" and he enjoys sharing the stories and experiences of our ancestors. In 2003 he received the national SAR Award for community service and outstanding citizenship.

Cover and Oil Paintings

Ron Goyette was one of Maine's foremost artists. His ability to capture the essence and heritage of New England's moods brought him national acclaim. His studio was in Kennebunkport, Maine.

Line Drawing

Claudia Crafts is a resident of Portsmouth, New Hampshire and a former art teacher. She specializes in watercolors and pen and ink drawings.

Bibliography

Finnegan, Kathleen E. and Harrison, Timothy E. <u>Lighthouses of Maine and New Hampshire</u>. Wells, ME: Lighthouse Digest, Inc., 1991.

Small, Constance Scovill. <u>The Lighthouse Keeper's Wife</u>. Orono: The University of Maine Press, 1986.

Snow, Edward Rowe. <u>Famous Lighthouses of New England</u>. Boston, MA: Yankee Publishing Co., 1945.

Sterling, Robert. <u>Lighthouses of the Maine Coast and the Men Who Keep Them</u>. Brattleboro, VT: Stephen Daye Press, 1935.

Thompson, Courtney. <u>Maine Lighthouses, A Pictorial Guide</u>. Mt. Desert, ME: Cat Nap Publications, 1996.

Thomson, William O. <u>A New England Lighthouse, The End of An Era</u>. Cape Neddick, ME: Nor'East Heritage Publications, 1986.